THRIVE!

Using Psalms to Help You Flourish

THRIVE!

Using Psalms to Help You Flourish

Douglas Jacoby

ILLUMINATION iP
PUBLISHERS

THRIVE!

Using Psalms to Help You Flourish
© 2014 by Douglas Jacoby

ISBN: 978-1-939086-79-2. Printed in the United States of America.

Unless otherwise indicated, all Scripture references are from the *Holy Bible*, New International Version, copyright ©1973, 1978, 1984, 2011 by Biblica, Inc. Used by permission. All rights reserved worldwide.

Scriptures marked RSV are from the *Revised Standard Version of the Bible*, copyright ©1946, 1952, and 1971 the Division of Christian Education of the National Council of the Churches of Christ in the United States of America. Used by permission. All rights reserved.

Scriptures marked ESV are from *The Holy Bible*, English Standard Version, copyright © 2001 by Crossway. Used by permission. All rights reserved.

Scriptures marked NLT are from the *Holy Bible, New Living Translation,* copyright © 1996, 2004, 2007 by Tyndale House Foundation. Used by permission of Tyndale House Publishers Inc. All rights reserved.

Scriptures marked NET are from the *NET Bible®* copyright ©1996-2006 by Biblical Studies Press, L.L.C. All rights reserved.

Interior book design: Douglas Jacoby
Cover design: Toney Mulhollan

Illumination Publishers, 6010 Pinecreek Ridge Court, Spring, Texas 77379-2513

www.ipibooks.com

TABLE OF CONTENTS

1

THRIVING—OR JUST SURVIVING? (PSALM 23)

You haven't been flourishing as a Christian for a while now. When people ask how you're doing, your response is an automatic "fine" or "okay"—blank words that don't reveal what you're really feeling...or maybe you don't know what you feel yourself. You find your real, inner self drifting in a sea of turmoil and uncertainty, with the Captain nowhere in sight. John of the Cross, in his *Dark Night of the Soul*, expressed the feeling in this way: "My spirit has become dry because it forgets to feed on You."[1] We've all been there.

The truth is that you've lost your spiritual anchor. You've wandered off the charted course you once navigated with purpose and focus; now you drift, unmoored and aimless, hoping the next storm won't pull you under.

Maybe you've been trying to hide your spiritual condition, but are you really fooling others anyway? Aren't many of *them* also experiencing this same melancholy? An unspoken agreement to keep things superficial guarantees that neither you nor they will ask the uncomfortable questions.

This dynamic is especially common among "middle-aged Christians," those who've been following the Lord for fifteen or twenty years or more but are slowly succumbing to spiritual suffocation (Luke 8:14).

You say this doesn't describe you? That's great. But even if your walk with God is thriving now, there may come a day when the outlook *isn't* so encouraging. One day you may feel a sense of hopelessness and find that your spirit, zeal, and joy need to be "restored."

Biblically speaking, restoration isn't only for those who have cut ties with fellow believers and gone back to the world. In the Bible, restoration is for those who have lost their first love for Christ and are now just "hanging in there"…just surviving (Galatians 6:1–2).

Psalm 23

¹ The LORD is my shepherd, I shall not be in want.

² He makes me lie down in green pastures,
  he leads me beside quiet waters,

³ he restores my soul.

He guides me in paths of righteousness
  for his name's sake.

⁴ Even though I walk
  through the valley of the shadow of death,

I will fear no evil,
  for you are with me;

your rod and your staff,
  they comfort me.

⁵ You prepare a table before me

> *in the presence of my enemies.*
> *You anoint my head with oil;*
> *my cup overflows.*
> [6] *Surely goodness and love will follow me*
> *all the days of my life,*
> *and I will dwell in the house of the LORD*
> *forever.*

Fortunately for us, the Lord is a good shepherd who restores our souls. Whose heart can fail to thrill at Jesus' beautiful declaration, so full of hope and promise? "I have come that they may have life, and have it to the full. I am the good shepherd" (John 10:10–11). There's always a way to get back on board, provided we're willing to grab the lifeline God throws us (1 Corinthians 10:12–13). The way back will require repentance—surrendering our lives to the Lord (again).

Does that sound difficult? It isn't. In another soaring promise, Jesus offers to help us when the way feels too rough and our burdens too heavy to carry alone:

> *"Come to me, all you who are weary and burdened, and I will give you rest. Take my yoke upon you and learn from me, for I am gentle and humble in heart, and you will find rest for your souls. For my yoke is easy and my burden is light."* (Matthew 11:28–30)

You can do this—you can rekindle the zeal you felt at first (1 John 5:3; Deuteronomy 30:11). The Lord has given us his promises and his word to get us back on track, to recapture our heart. And when it comes to reaching the heart, no other book in Scripture is quite like Psalms.

Christians are encouraged to use the book of Psalms as a constant, nourishing part of our spiritual life, in worship and communion with God (Ephesians 5:18–19; Colossians 3:15–16). From the opening verse of Psalm 1, "Blessed is the man…," to the closing exhortation of Psalm 150, "Let everything that has breath praise the Lord," readers throughout the ages have found comfort and restoration for their souls.

In a sense, Psalms has always been the hymnbook and the prayer book of the church. The psalms are rich and deep. They touch our hearts, revealing the inner emotions and currents.

Our hearts may be filled with heartache, chaos, and contradiction. And when the waters of life and spirituality become murky or rough, we may not need a list of things to do, a "how-to" book, or a new code of discipline. Sometimes we just need connection—a lifeline that we can cling to and follow back to safety—back to God. The psalms don't offer solutions to all our problems so much as they offer therapy—thoughts and emotions to which we can all relate.

Of course, restoration will require effort and focus, but it is refreshing. In the end, it means fervor and life (Psalm 51:12; Romans 12:11; Revelation 3:14–20).

When you first came to faith you were aglow with God's Spirit. God *was* real and he *felt* real. No matter what you have been through in your spiritual journey, no matter how far off course you may have drifted or how long you have been lost at sea, know this: God is as real today as he was when you first started out.

> **The psalms don't offer solutions to problems so much as they offer therapy.**

So much has happened since your early days. Even if you have gotten discouraged and found yourself drifting, this need not be the end of your story. Once again our hearts can be reignited with heavenly fire. The book of Psalms can be the life raft God uses to guide us back to our first love. If you've been spiritually floundering, it's time to stop treading water, simply surviving; let the psalms redirect, restore, and revive you—it's never too late to *thrive*.

Heart questions

- Am I reading this book as a self-improvement plan? Do I realize that a relationship with God is infinitely more than a new spiritual plan or a to-do list?

- What are my expectations about the Lord strengthening me through the psalms? Are they high or low—and why?

- Is there any sense in which my faith needs to be reignited—to "be rekindled with fire from above"?

Prayer points

- To be honest in speech, not pretending to be doing better than I really am (Acts 5:1–11).

- To make the most of fellowship, renouncing superficiality, truly caring how others are doing (Colossians 1:28–2:1).

- Not merely to survive but, in Christ, to thrive (John 10:10).

---

[1] St. John of the Cross (1542–1591), *Dark Night of the Soul.* Available at www.ccel.org/ccel/john_cross.

2
TWO PATHS (PSALM 1)

Ancient Jews and Christians loved to sing psalms and make music, not only in worship, but on most every occasion. They loved the full range of emotions and thoughts they could encounter as they celebrated, contemplated, sang, hummed, chanted, and memorized the psalms.

The evidence for this infatuation is enormous. Psalms is the book of the Old Testament most quoted in the New Testament—more than 100 times.[2] Even in the Dead Sea Scrolls, Psalms occupies pride of place.

Psalm 1 is the introduction to the entire Psalter, the collection of psalms. Like the Torah (the books of Genesis through Deuteronomy), Psalms has been arranged into five books, each with a different emphasis (though that's beyond the purpose of our book[3]).

Book I	Psalms 1–41
Book II	Psalms 42–72
Book III	Psalms 73–89
Book IV	Psalms 90–106
Book V	Psalms 107–150

Obedience is one thing; having one's heart in it is another. While the Torah was concerned with people's actions (Deuteronomy 4:1–6, 13–14; 30:11–14), in many passages it also touched on motivations of the heart (Leviticus 19:17–18). Yet in most of the Torah we don't peer into the inner life. The law was given, and it was up to God's followers to implement it. Psalms deals more with the interior life—the heart, mind, and soul.

Although psalms have lyrics—they are poetry sung to the accompaniment of a plucked instrument[4] (like a harp or lyre)—you'll probably notice a huge amount of variety within the Psalter. Psalm 1 resembles Proverbs. That's because it's a Wisdom Psalm (like Psalms 14, 19, 25, 49, and many others). Here, each stanza contains a proverb.

Psalm 1 will help us to be wise. Yet to be wise, we must walk in the way of the wise. Wisdom isn't the same thing as knowledge. It's spiritual, and it begins with knowledge of God. Wisdom is more than intellect; it's making right choices. That's what is meant by "walk." Walking has to do with how we live in the real world—no fairyland, no pretending.

The first psalm, as we will see, is practical—nothing fluffy here. Get with the program and find the right path, the psalmist tells us. But there's more to this psalm than just its six verses. Each psalm connects to other psalms—sometimes to those immediately before or after them in the Psalter, other times to psalms far removed. The connections may not always be obvious, but when you understand them, they cast new light on the psalms and add much to your appreciation of them.

Psalm 1 exhibits several such connections. The second psalm illustrates the rejection of God's rule in the world (the way of the wicked, which is also referenced in Psalm 1): everyone is up in arms, rejecting God's rightful sovereignty. Further, the prayer of Psalm 25 expounds on Psalm 1. (You will also notice that Psalm 1, unlike most psalms, isn't a prayer at all.) It's not just about making smart choices, but about prayer, passion, and petition.

Psalm 1

¹ Blessed is the man
   who walks not in the counsel of the wicked,
nor stands in the way of sinners,
   nor sits in the seat of scoffers;
² but his delight is in the law of the LORD,
   and on his law he meditates day and night.
³ He is like a tree
   planted by streams of water,
that yields its fruit in its season,
   and its leaf does not wither.
In all that he does, he prospers.
⁴ The wicked are not so,
   but are like chaff which the wind drives away.
⁵ Therefore the wicked will not stand in the judgment,
   nor sinners in the congregation of the righteous;
⁶ for the LORD knows the way of the righteous,
   but the way of the wicked will perish. RSV

The psalms encompass poetry *and* reality. We see from the opening of the book of Psalms, regardless of the many emotions to be explored in these 150 chapters, that the real world still has some hard edges. Our feelings may be subjective, but that doesn't mean everything is relative.

> **Although the psalms explore subjective feelings, reality isn't subjective. It has some hard edges!**

There are still only two paths: the way of wisdom and the way of folly. Good and evil, righteousness and wickedness. The world may prefer that there be three ways, or four—or seven billion. But wishing doesn't make it so.

Although one path is more popular than the other (Matthew 7:13–14), God asks you and me to separate ourselves from the crowd. We shouldn't kid ourselves about this. If we buy in to the relativistic pabulum served up by the media, we're in for a rude awakening. Sooner or later we will bump our head into the hard contours of reality!

By spending time in Psalms we become wise. We move in the right direction, and we make better choices. Notice that 1:2 mentions the Torah, and 1:3 alludes to the prophets (Jeremiah 17:7–8). Walking with God means we're into his word, processing his wisdom. Listen to God's word (v2), not to the world (1 John 4:5; 1 Corinthians 1:20, 3:19, 15:33). There are consequences either way: we flourish or we wither.

The wicked wither because they aren't rooted. The righteous prosper. This prospering (vitality) should *never* be confused with the false promises of modern prosperity theology. ("Put God first, and you will get the pay raise/get the girl/receive healing/have an easy life…") The Hebrew idea of prosperity is much simpler. It didn't involve tons of money, but rather the meeting of life's *basic* needs: successful crops, the gift of children and grandchildren, and achieving a respected place in the community. In a nutshell, it's Matthew 6:25–34, a passage that has been sorely twisted by the prosperity gospel movement.

Why do the wicked vanish? They lack solidity. They cannot stand. They are lightweights! Their punishment (being blown away) is a natural result of their waywardness, not something arbitrary or artificial. Outcomes, results, consequences—this is how the Lord, more often than not, works in our lives.

Stop looking for separate rewards or punishments—until the judgment day—and look around. What's happening in your life right now? The outworking of God's righteous judgment takes place every day. Psalm 7:11, Romans 1:18–21, Proverbs 10:30–31, and many other passages illustrate this truth. Similarly, prosperity is more a result of righteous living over time than a reward. The olive tree, so common in Palestine (Psalm 128:3), bears fruit for centuries, usually in alternate years. Even if the main trunk dies, it still sends up shoots. And so it thrives. The tree planted by streams of water in verse 3 alludes to the Tree of Life in Genesis 2–3.

Daily bread

Notice in this psalm that the bad guys don't give a thought for God. The good guys think about him and his law not only every day, but throughout most of the day as well. It's like Israel and the manna (Exodus 16). The Israelites had to go out every day and collect the manna from heaven, and they had to do it in the morning, before the heat of the day set in and burned it away. I like the way Chinese missionary Hudson Taylor put it: "Do not have your concert first, and then tune your instrument afterwards. Begin the day with the Word of God and prayer, and get first of all into harmony with Him."

Are we setting aside time on a daily basis to collect the "manna" the Lord has given us, and do we continue to feast on it throughout the day? If not, we are probably becoming spiritually weak. Besides the manna story, be sure to look at Deuteronomy 8:3 and Matthew 4:4, because Jesus thought this was a vital lesson for us all.

> **Are we setting aside time on a daily basis to collect the "manna" the Lord has given us?**

When I came to faith in Christ, the older Christians in my new church family urged me to set aside time for a daily devotional, or "quiet time."

I took the admonition seriously. I hadn't been brought up in the church or with faith, and I didn't know any Bible when I started on my spiritual journey. That was some 15,000 daily devotionals ago. It all adds up, and looking back, I can see the way faith has accumulated over the years, as each day has built upon the one before. I'm so glad I listened to the advice of those wise Christians in my early days! It's absolutely been worth it.

If you are a brother or sister who needs to make a decision about your daily walk with the Lord, don't delay any longer. There are tremendous benefits in developing the discipline of setting aside time to be with the Lord to not only jump start your day, but to provide "spiritual bread" to nourish you through the day (Deuteronomy 8:3; Joshua 1:8; Proverbs 8:34; Psalm 42:2).

On a personal note, let me tell you why I'm writing a book on Psalms, especially since many brothers and sisters in Christ are more qualified than I. At about the ten-year mark in my Christian walk, I realized that I was usually reading through the Bible once a year. I remember hearing a guest speaker who shared that on his present trajectory, he would read through the Bible fifty times by the time he died. That stuck with me.

Not only did I begin to intentionally finish the Bible every year, but by the time I was fifteen years in the Lord, I began challenging other disciples to consider doing the same. On one of my trips to India, I shared this idea. When I returned to India the next year, I was stunned to find that all the Christian leaders had taken up the challenge—those with a high degree of education *and* those who had never finished even secondary school. And they were excited about the experience! Their enthusiasm fueled me to continue this practice in my own life and to continue sharing it wherever I travel to speak.

Yet by the time I'd read the whole Bible fifty times, I felt like I needed a change. A brother whom I respect had made a practice of praying through Psalms—much like the early church or the medieval monks—and his example encouraged me. The next year (2012), the book of Psalms was *all* I read. Once a week I read/prayed through all 150 psalms. (I was "doubling up" on prayer and Bible study!) I found that my heart was invigorated and inspired in ways I had not anticipated—my walk with God reached new levels of zeal and closeness. The idea for this book emerged from that experience, and these pages reflect the lessons and faith and growth that were the psalms' gift to me.

Now I'm back to reading the whole Bible once a year (usually completing it in the spring), followed by more focused studies of particular biblical books and themes. Although I have a fairly broad grasp of Scripture, I realize I still have so much room for improvement—for growth—that my lifelong endeavor to saturate myself in Scripture will never conclude. The ocean is deep!

There are only two paths. Do you want to stay on the right path? To flourish? To thrive? I doubt you're all that different from me. You aren't satisfied with where you are. You long for consistency; you long for more; you don't want to "slip" (Psalm 37:31).

There's a restlessness in your bones, and you want to

A Dozen Reasons for Daily Devotions

1. Starting the day communing with the Lord

2. Creating a spiritual focus for the entire day

3. Breaking the fleshly habits of undisciplined wasting of time: going to bed late, watching television, obsessively checking emails and texting, etc.

4. Beginning the day in a less pressured manner

5. Setting better priorities

6. Being stronger spiritually

7. Fighting temptation with Scripture

8. Gaining a broader, deeper grasp of the big story of Scripture

9. Having more to share with seekers and believers alike

10. Keeping a clear conscience

11. Tuning in to the leading of the Spirit

12. Developing the mind of Christ

understand the Word, think God's thoughts, live a life of adventure guided by Scripture. Yet the Lord won't force us. It's our decision. The adventurous path is waiting for us—won't you step onto that path with me? As a later psalm puts it, "I run in the path of your commands, for you have set my heart free" (Psalm 119:32).

As Peter Craigie so beautifully wrote, "The essence of the road of the righteous is this: it is a road too difficult to walk without the companionship and friendship of God. The psalmist, troubled from without and within, has stopped for a moment in the way; he knows he cannot turn back, but scarcely knows how to continue. And so he prays that God would show him the road and make him walk in it."[5]

Every psalm has something for us, beginning with the first. Meditate on Psalm 1. Memorize it. Listen to a podcast.[6] Read it in multiple versions. Share a verse with a friend. The psalm and the seed of its message will burrow into your heart, helping you, in turn, to extend your spiritual roots ever deeper. The deeper the roots go, the higher the tree can grow.

Heart questions

- How rooted am I? Do I flit from one thing to another, or am I anchored in the Word and willing to do the work?
- How productive am I? Am I getting things done? Am I helping others to know Christ? Do I look for ways to serve others, especially those in need?
- Have I fully accepted the truth of the *two ways*, or am I

trying too hard not to give offense, to appear neutral?

- Do I meditate on the Word daily? What are my devotional habits, and how might they need to change?

Prayer points

- To be captivated by the wisdom of God and the word of God, not impressed by the things of the world or by people the world idolizes.
- To be solid, stable, and productive—not to wither.
- To accept that there are only two paths—and not to be double-minded or wishy-washy about this.
- To go in confidence.
- To be filled with the power and wisdom of the Holy Spirit.

---

[2] See http://www.jesuswalk.com/psalms/psalms-NT-quotations.htm.

[3] Most of the Psalms in Book I refer to God as *Yahweh* (usually rendered LORD, in distinction to *Elohim*, rendered God). Book II contains mainly psalms of David or the Korahites, while most of the entries in Book III are by Asaph or the Korahites. Book III also has a strong concern with Jerusalem and the Temple. Book IV contains mainly anonymous psalms of praise and thanksgiving, as does Book V. Book V also has Praise Psalms (111–118, 145–150) and Psalms of Ascent (120–134). Psalms 146–150 serve as the conclusion to the Psalter, just as Psalm 1 (some commentators would say 1–2) serves as the introduction.

[4] The ancient Greek *psallo* meant pluck.

[5] Peter C. Craigie, in the *Word Biblical Commentary Vol. 19, Psalms 1–50*, 222.

[6] www.douglasjacoby.com/ps1. Many other Psalms podcasts are available too, for a total of ten in the initial series, and eight more by my Filipino colleague in the teaching ministry, Rolan Monje.

3
GOD'S WORD IN THE PSALMS
(PSALMS 19 AND 119)

"I bow down toward your holy temple and give thanks to your name for your steadfast love and your faithfulness, for you have exalted above all things your name and your word" (Psalm 138:2 ESV). What a majestic verse! If we're going to enjoy our life in Christ and live wisely, there are two places to focus: God's name and his word.

- God's *name* means who he is (as in Exodus 33:18–19, 34:6–7, the fullest statements of the nature and character of God in the entire Bible). His name isn't a handle or a password, or even a personal name (YHWH in the Hebrew consonants). Maybe in one sense Yahweh is his name, in that it's Hebrew for I AM. Since God always exists, he is the Great I AM, or I AM WHO I AM (Exodus 3:14). Yet to learn of his identity, deeds, and will—everything entailed in his name—we'll need to spend some serious time in his word.

- His *word* indicates his will, the truth found in God. "The words of the Lord are pure words, like silver refined in a furnace on the ground, purified seven times" (Psalm 12:6 ESV). What God says is true, trustworthy, and precious.

It's hard to take seriously anyone who claims respect for God but can't be bothered to investigate his word, any more than we would seek treatment from a doctor who hasn't read a journal since med school.

Yet are there two "words of God"? We find the word of God in the Bible,[7] which is God's written message to us humans. And Jesus is the Word. When "the Word became flesh" (John 1:14), God became flesh, incarnate. The Bible didn't become incarnate, and Jesus obviously isn't the Bible. There are various parallels between the Word who became flesh and the word that became paper. (Maybe I should have said papyrus or parchment. You know what I mean.) We won't pursue those parallels now, though they're intriguing.

We can worship Christ, because in nature he is God. Yet we don't worship the Bible—the form of idolatry called bibliolatry. Nevertheless, by immersing ourselves in Scripture, we are able to learn God's good and perfect will for our lives (Romans 12:2): what sorts of people we should be striving to become, how we are to live out our faith, and what it means to have Christ living in us by faith.

The important thing is to have the right attitude towards the written Word, just as we strive for the right disposition towards the incarnate Word. In Psalm 138, God's word refers to his expressed will—available in Scripture. In the pages of the Bible, we meet the Lord. "As in Paradise, God walks in Scripture, seeking man."[8]

Although we don't worship the Bible, it's beyond dispute that our worship of God is accelerated when the word of Christ is dwelling in us richly (Colossians 3:16).

> **"As in Paradise, God walks in Scripture, seeking man."**

Though several psalms showcase the word of God, let's focus on the two most conspicuous: Psalms 19 and 119.

Psalm 19

¹ The heavens declare the glory of God;
*   the skies proclaim the work of his hands.*
² Day after day they pour forth speech;
*   night after night they reveal knowledge.*
³ They have no speech, they use no words;
*   no sound is heard from them.*
⁴ Yet their voice goes out into all the earth,
*   their words to the ends of the world.*
In the heavens God has pitched a tent for the sun.
⁵ It is like a bridegroom coming out of his chamber,
*   like a champion rejoicing to run his course.*
⁶ It rises at one end of the heavens
*   and makes its circuit to the other;*
*   nothing is deprived of its warmth.*

⁷ *The law of the LORD is perfect,*
   refreshing the soul.
The statutes of the LORD are trustworthy,
   making wise the simple.
⁸ *The precepts of the LORD are right,*
   giving joy to the heart.
The commands of the LORD are radiant,
   giving light to the eyes.
⁹ *The fear of the LORD is pure,*
   enduring forever.
The decrees of the LORD are firm,
   and all of them are righteous.
¹⁰ *They are more precious than gold,*
   than much pure gold;
they are sweeter than honey,
   than honey from the honeycomb.
¹¹ *By them your servant is warned;*
   in keeping them there is great reward.
¹² *But who can discern their own errors?*
   Forgive my hidden faults.
¹³ *Keep your servant also from willful sins;*
   may they not rule over me.
Then I will be blameless,
   innocent of great transgression.
¹⁴ *May these words of my mouth and this meditation of my heart*
   be pleasing in your sight,
   LORD, my Rock and my Redeemer.

According to this psalm, God reveals himself in two ways, in two books: his book of works, nature (vv1–6) and his book of words, Scripture (vv7–11). The psalm is capped off with a prayer (like 139:23–24), one which cuts to the heart of who we are and why we do what we do (vv12–14). The final phrase in verse 14 is the declaration that our God is *real* and *solid*, unlike the shadowy apparitions and manmade idols the pagans worshipped. No wonder C. S. Lewis considers Psalm 19 one of the greatest lyrics ever penned.[9]

> **According to the Bible itself, God speaks in two "books." One is his book of works, nature; the other is his book of words, Scripture.**

Of course, God communicates with us in multiple ways—not solely through Scripture. And this is according to the Bible itself (Hebrews 1:1). He speaks through the person of Christ, the history of Israel, experience, wise counselors, answered prayer, and (as Psalm 19 so eloquently illustrates) *nature*.

One reason I love science—whether looking into a telescope, catching up on the latest in biology, or even having my mind stretched by the paradoxes of physics—is that the experience verges on worship.[10] I am amazed by the creation, which itself assures me that there is a Creator. "To the sensitive, the heavenly praise of God's glory may be an overwhelming experience, whereas to the insensitive, sky is simply sky and stars are only stars; they point to nothing beyond."[11]

Incidentally, since the God who speaks to us in nature is the Creator and true author of science, we can be sure that any contradiction between Scripture and science stems from our limited understanding: the result of misreading the Bible or maybe misreading nature. The two are equally valid as vehicles of revelation. Another passage supporting this idea is Romans 1:19–20:

For what may be known about God is plain to them, because God has shown it to them. For God's invisible attributes, namely, his eternal power and divine nature, have been clearly perceived, ever since the creation of the world, in the things that have been made. (ESV)

The Bible's unique attitude toward nature may escape us modern readers. The ancient world was abounding in gods and goddesses representing various natural elements and powers. People worshiped solar deities. . . and yet we find no hymns to sun gods in the Bible. Instead of nature being deified—which would mean idolatry (Romans 1:25; Ezekiel 8:15–16)—the Bible tells us that nature itself praises God (vv1, 5). In Genesis 1 and many similar texts, the Bible draws a sharp delineation between Creator and creation, and this view set Judaism apart in the ancient world.

Notice the key terms in the psalm, different ways of referring to the Word: law, statutes, precepts, commands, fear, and decrees. Fear may seem the odd one out, until we consider that the fear of the Lord is the beginning of wisdom (Psalm 111:10; Proverbs 1:7; Job 28:28).

> **Great are the works of the Lord,**
> **studied by all who delight in them.**
> Psalm 111:2 ESV

Do we want to be refreshed, wise, joyful, radiant, consistent, and holy? Then we need the Word in our lives. The end result is that *our* words, like our actions, thoughts, and motivations, will be true and pure—just like our heavenly Father.

Psalm 119

The longest chapter in the longest book of the Bible is entirely structured around a single theme: God's word. This 176-verse, 22-stanza poem/prayer is an overwhelming tribute to the truth, power, and vitality of Scripture. Several of the psalm's potent passages appear in the "Prayer points" below.

The psalm is also an acrostic. That means that each successive verse begins with the next letter in the Hebrew alphabet. (There are twenty-two consonants in all, from *alef* to *tav*—thus 22 stanzas of 8 verses each = 176 verses in all.) The other acrostic psalms are 9–10 (which were originally one psalm), 25, 34, 37, 111, 112, and 145.

For some Bible readers, Psalm 119 feels repetitive to the point of dullness. However, I suspect it isn't the fault of the psalm or the psalmist; it's our own dullness. The more spiritually alive we are, the more the psalm speaks to us. When we are sensitized to the Lord's presence and to centering our lives round his commands, there is nothing superfluous about this psalm—rather, we appreciate its nuances. I have read (actually prayed) Psalm 119 more than a hundred times, and I never fail to find something new. God always speaks to my heart.

Let's take a closer look at just a few lines from this majestic psalm. At first glance, they may seem similar—mere echoes of the same theme—but when you dive in to explore the details and subtleties of the language, you see how they celebrate different aspects of God's word and help us to appreciate its many subtle shades in Technicolor:

Verse 24 says, "Your statutes are my delight; they are my counselors." God's word is meant to thrill our very soul—to bring exquisite joy. And not only that, it counsels us, guiding us like a wise friend through life's decisions.

Verse 50 reveals a different role the Scriptures play in our lives: "My comfort in my suffering is this: Your promise preserves my life." God's word comforts us in times of difficulty and loss, suffering and confusion. It gives us the sense of security and safety that only the truth can provide. What a comfort it is to *know* that we are walking the right path, the straight path, the path of promise that guards our life, not only here in our earthly bodies, but throughout eternity.

And then there's the beautiful verse 54: "Your decrees are the theme of my song wherever I lodge." When we're spiritually thriving, God's words are the music of our heart, the soundtrack of our life, wherever we go.

In every one of the 176 verses of this psalm, we find priceless gems like these, packed with wisdom and joy, just waiting to be unearthed and enjoyed. As the psalm goes on, the writer rejoices in God's multifaceted law, longs for consistency, and prays that others will come to God as the Word guides his life on the right path. We may not be required to follow Torah—we are bound to the Lord through a *new* covenant—but still, nearly everything in Psalm 119 is relevant to the Christian life. The more we take these words into our hearts, the greater our love for God's word will become, until we, like the psalmist, can say, "Oh, how I love your law! I meditate on it all day long" (v97).

Heart questions

- Am I willing to become a careful reader—are my eyes fully open?

- Am I doing what I need to do to ensure that my heart is captivated by God's word, and not the world?

- How strong is the connection between *God's* word, truthfulness, integrity, will, nature, and so on, and *mine*? Am I putting the Word into my heart?

Prayer points

(from Psalm 119:10, 18, 36, 37, 112, 133, 176 ESV)

- Let me not wander from your commandments.

- Open my eyes that I may see wonderful things in your word.

- Incline my heart to your testimonies, and not to selfish gain.

- Turn my eyes from looking at worthless things; and give me life in your ways.

- Incline my heart to perform your statutes forever, to the end.

- Keep me steady according to your promise, and let no iniquity get dominion over me.

- I have gone astray like a lost sheep; seek your servant, for I do not forget your commandments.

---

[7] Although Christians say, "The Bible is God's word," that affirmation is a deduction, more than a biblical doctrine, technically speaking.

[8] Ambrose of Milan (330–397 AD), *De Paradiso*.

[9] C. S. Lewis, *Reflections on the Psalms* online pdf, www.scribd.com /doc/27582307/C-S-Lewis-Reflections-on-the-Psalms), 56.

[10] For more on this, watch my student resource DVD *Science and Faith: Enemies or Allies?* (Spring, Texas: IPI, 2013).

[11] Craigie, in the *Word Biblical Commentary Vol. 19, Psalms 1–50*, 181.

4
FINDING GOD IN THE PSALMS
(PSALMS 130 AND 103)

So far we have seen that to thrive, we need to take the right
path—and this means following the word of God. Yet it's not
some sort of mechanical process. It's about God. The Bible is
a book about relationship: who we are, how we relate to the
Lord, and how we relate to others.

Since our purpose is to know God and bring glory to
him, we are wise to turn our attention, in this chapter, to the
nature of the true God. Please read through the two psalms
selected for this purpose, unhurriedly—let them sink in. Then
contemplate the salient points about our Lord. My brevity (just
seven points) doesn't mean I ran out of ideas or the psalms ran
out of steam. Rather, the suggestions are to get us thinking.
Anyone who spends considerable time in the Word will be able
to expand the list.

Like the closing of Psalm 19, the beginning of Psalm
130 is humbling. It puts us in our place: on our knees in the
presence of an awesome yet gracious God.

Psalm 130

¹ Out of the depths I cry to you, LORD;
  ² Lord, hear my voice.
Let your ears be attentive
    to my cry for mercy.
³ If you, LORD, kept a record of sins,
    Lord, who could stand?
⁴ But with you there is forgiveness,
    so that we can, with reverence, serve you.
⁵ I wait for the LORD, my whole being waits,
    and in his word I put my hope.
⁶ I wait for the Lord
    more than watchmen wait for the morning,
    more than watchmen wait for the morning.
⁷ Israel, put your hope in the LORD,
    for with the LORD is unfailing love
    and with him is full redemption.
⁸ He himself will redeem Israel
    from all their sins.

No record of sins—full redemption? What a glorious promise of God we have to lean on! Similar to Psalm 130 is Psalm 103, another exquisite piece of the Bible. (The 1-3-0 and 1-0-3 are mnemonically handy—as with 73 and 37, upcoming in chapter 7—although there's no theological significance, since chapter and verse numbers aren't inspired.)

Psalm 103

¹ Bless the LORD, O my soul,
* and all that is within me,*
* bless his holy name.*
² Bless the LORD, O my soul,
* and do not forget all his benefits—*
³ who forgives all your iniquity,
* who heals all your diseases,*
⁴ who redeems your life from the Pit,
* who crowns you with steadfast love and mercy,*
⁵ who satisfies you with good as long as you live
* so that your youth is renewed like the eagle's.*
⁶ The LORD works vindication
* and justice for all who are oppressed.*
⁷ He made known his ways to Moses,
* his acts to the people of Israel.*
⁸ The LORD is merciful and gracious,
* slow to anger and abounding in steadfast love.*
⁹ He will not always accuse,
* nor will he keep his anger forever.*
¹⁰ He does not deal with us according to our sins,
* nor repay us according to our iniquities.*
¹¹ For as the heavens are high above the earth,
* so great is his steadfast love toward those who fear him;*
¹² as far as the east is from the west,
* so far he removes our transgressions from us.*
¹³ As a father has compassion for his children,

so the LORD has compassion for those who fear him.
14 For he knows how we were made;
he remembers that we are dust.
15 As for mortals, their days are like grass;
they flourish like a flower of the field;
16 for the wind passes over it, and it is gone,
and its place knows it no more.
17 But the steadfast love of the LORD is from everlasting to
everlasting on those who fear him,
and his righteousness to children's children,
18 to those who keep his covenant
and remember to do his commandments.
19 The LORD has established his throne in the heavens,
and his kingdom rules over all.
20 Bless the LORD, O you his angels,
you mighty ones who do his bidding,
obedient to his spoken word.
21 Bless the LORD, all his hosts,
his ministers that do his will.
22 Bless the LORD, all his works,
in all places of his dominion.
Bless the LORD, O my soul. NRSV

At least seven qualities of God emerge from the psalms. Most of these can be located in the two offerings above, though I'll provide a few more passages in case you want to study each trait in more depth.

I. Power

His power is unspeakable, without equal and beyond all comparison. "Great is our Lord and mighty in power; his understanding has no limit" (147:5; also 18:1–2, 20:7).

II. Sovereignty

My favorite passage on his sovereignty is: "Our God is in heaven! He does whatever he pleases!" (115:3 NET; also 57:5, 11; 103:19; 113:4). We have no right to challenge him. *He* is Lord—not you or I.

III. Solidity (reality)

Just as the wicked are "lightweights" (Psalm 1:4), so their gods are phantoms. But the true God is hefty, substantial. "The Lord is my rock, my fortress and my deliverer; my God is my rock…" (18:2; also 19:14). He's solid, real.

IV. Superiority

Yahweh is superior to all rivals. The false gods have to be carried around, since they're powerless even to move. "Praise be to the Lord, to God our Savior, who daily bears our burdens" (68:19). The pagan deities are useless in helping you and me with our burdens. As they had to be carried, *they were* the burden! (Also Psalm 96, and for a few laughs, 1 Samuel 5:2–4; 1 Kings 18:26–39.)

V. Mercy

The Lord is full of *chesed*, a key word in the Hebrew Old Testament meaning love, loving-kindness, and mercy. "The Lord is gracious and compassionate, slow to anger and rich in love. The Lord is good to all; he has compassion on all he has made" (145:8–9; also 100:5, 103:8–13, 117:2). And *because* he is faithful, we can trust in his mercy.

VI. Praiseworthiness

"Praise the Lord. How good it is to sing praises to our God, how pleasant and fitting to praise him!" (147:1). We rightly thank God when he meets our needs (as in 107:9), but praise isn't the same as thanks. When we praise God, we honor him for his intrinsic excellence (qualities of holiness, justice, goodness, wisdom, power, mercy, and much more)—not just for how he has touched our lives. I found *ninety* psalms encouraging us to praise the Lord!

VII. Availability

It's a stunning thought that the Lord of the universe is available whenever we want to connect with him. When we're not really connected, we languish. We grow thirsty, even faint (Psalms 63, 61, and 84). All too often, we let "the worries of this life and the deceitfulness of wealth" distract us from taking the time to make this all-important connection—and in those times, we begin to flounder (Matthew 13:22). Fortunately, "the Lord is near to all who call on him, to all who call on him in truth" (145:18).

This is no trivial connection. We dare not approach his throne with deceit in our hearts. He answers when we call on him *in truth*—think of what Jesus said to the Samaritan woman in John 4:24. (Also see Psalms 42:2; 73:28; 84:2, 10; 105:4.) Sometimes the problem isn't that we are insincere or dishonest. We may be downcast, depressed, dejected (Psalm 42–43[12]). Or we may even have an attitude towards God, preferring he leave us alone (39:13; also Job 10:20; 1 Kings 19:3–5)—ever felt that way?

Once again, these are only seven of Yahweh's aspects. A most meager attempt—a miserable explanation, in light of the utter vastness of his awesomeness. Even though his paths are beyond tracing out (Romans 11:33), I attempted it anyway. And of course I failed—I admit it freely. We all fail when we try to "explain God," or summarize him in theological disquisition. And "disquisition"—what kind of a word is that? We think we're so clever. But God is omniscient! (Psalm 147:5).

Fruitlessness, failure, and faith

Let's admit it: We don't always connect with God. We don't even always *want* to connect with him. (Are we nuts? The Lord of the cosmos cares about me—a bug?—and I'm not reciprocating?)

There are all sorts of reasons (mainly excuses) why we don't pray. One of them deserves to be exposed. And it *is* exposed, in a psalm most Bible readers don't realize is a psalm. Actually, there are quite a few psalms in the Bible outside the

Things that can lure us away from the Lord

Television, novels, music, and other entertainment
Electronic devices
Excessive social media
Drugs (legal or illegal)
Unspiritual friends
Peer pressure to follow sports
Peer pressure to follow fashion
Obsession with health or exercise
Overly busy schedules
Self-pity
Ingratitude and blindness to blessings

Psalter, some of them extremely ancient. There are at least seven psalms before Psalms: the Song of the Sea (Exodus 15:1–18), the Song of the Ark (Numbers 10:35–36), the Oracles of Balaam (Numbers 23–24), the Song of Moses (Deuteronomy 32), the Blessing of Moses (Deuteronomy 33), the Song of Deborah (Judges 5), and the Song of Hannah (1 Samuel 2:1–10).[13] So the next psalm we will explore is found long after Psalm 150. In fact, it comes along 390 chapters later, smack in the middle of the Minor Prophets.

Habakkuk 3 is a splendid psalm/prayer set in a period when things looked bleak for Israel. These were not happy times. Life seemed ridiculously unfair, the pagan Babylonians were prospering instead of the Israelites, and even believing in God was colossally challenging. Let's zoom in on the last few verses.

Though the fig tree does not bud
  and there are no grapes on the vines,
though the olive crop fails
  and the fields produce no food,
though there are no sheep in the pen
  and no cattle in the stalls,
yet I will rejoice in the LORD,
  I will be joyful in God my Savior.
The Sovereign LORD is my strength;
  he makes my feet like the feet of a deer,
  he enables me to tread on the heights.

(Habakkuk 3:17–19)

We cannot—must not—base our relationship with God on our success or productivity. Because sometimes things will go great, but other times we may find ourselves in a "drier" period. Our salvation, and even our joy, should not fluctuate wildly, according to the kind of day we're having or the degree of success we're experiencing in our personal life or ministry. We should be confident to approach God even when things are slow and we could be tempted to feel like failures.

To tie our faithfulness and joy to results is immature, humanistic and, as Habakkuk shows us, unbiblical. It's also counterproductive and makes prayer burdensome—and if we're not careful, it will steal our joy and usher us into that bleak wilderness of spiritual survival. If you've been barely surviving in your spiritual walk, take a look at where you've sought your joy and faith. Even in the midst of failure, we are still called to faith. And if we have found the true and living God, he won't leave us floundering. He will enable us to live our lives with Christian confidence and Christlike joy.

> **We cannot—we must not—base our relationship with God on our success or productivity.**

In the psalms we find God, and the encounter is breathtaking, life-changing. We find God not just in the first 150 psalms, but in all of the psalms throughout the Bible. Knowing the Lord is what the Christian life is all about. It's not about knowledge per se, but about relationship (1 Corinthians 8:1–3). If this is our perspective, the study of Psalms will continue to show us the object of our longing—the One by whom and for whom we were created.

Heart questions

- Do I long to be with the Lord?
- Is there sometimes a part of me that wants the Lord to go away?
- Do I appreciate the radical difference between the biblical God and the so-called gods of our world?
- Do I feel that I need mercy, or am I more like the self-righteous Pharisee of Luke 18 or the merciless servant of Matthew 18?
- Do I praise God for who he is, or is my tendency merely to thank him when he blesses me?
- Do I tend to measure the quality of my relationship with God by results?

Prayer points

- Lord, may I be awed by you, not by the things of this world.
- Lord, help me to be like the deer that pants for the water, even when my soul is downcast.
- Lord, rebuke in me the thought that I can ever stand by my own righteousness.
- Lord, let my soul be wholly enamored of you—not in it for what I can get, but because of who you are.

---

[12] In the original Hebrew, Psalms 42 and 43 are a single psalm. The same is true of Psalms 9 and 10.

[13] Craigie, in the *Word Biblical Commentary Vol. 19, Psalms 1–50*, 25.

5

DOUBLE FOCUS (PSALMS 40 AND 117)

As we observed in chapter 2, the Old Testament didn't require robotic conformity, nor was it obsessed with outward behavior. God cares about our entire being. The psalms make it even easier to grasp this concept, illustrating it in a variety of ways (1:2, 19:14, 139:23–24, 145:17–18). Consider also 141:3–4: "Set a guard over my mouth, Lord; keep watch over the door of my lips. Do not let my heart be drawn to what is evil."

The psalms shed light on the heart, and direct us to focus at two levels: inward and outward. In this chapter we'll explore this simple idea.

Not all the psalms are as straightforward as Psalm 1. Most dwell at length on the full range of human emotions—especially sadness or bewilderment. Perhaps forty percent of the psalms deal with loss, mourning, or despondency. As a result, they may ramble, skip around, or not be as elegantly constructed as we might wish. Don't worry if you don't follow every logical leap or grasp every connection. The psalms weren't written by engineers.

Yet there is an even deeper consideration—and one that should help us to appreciate the character of Scripture even as it helps us resolve a number of "Bible contradictions." While in much of the Bible God speaks to us humans, in the psalms, the direction is reversed. Here *we* are speaking to God, sharing the good, the bad, and even the ugly that hides within the human heart. While we should not always embrace the theology of the psalms—remember, they are written by people, confessing their inmost thoughts, even their sinful ones—we should certainly imitate their realness. Without honesty, there is no authenticity, and our religion runs the risk of losing touch with reality. Without honesty, we cannot find the intimate connection with God we long for. We will return to the theme of (brutal) honesty in chapter 9.

> **Psalms encourages us to work through negative feelings—to get honest with God.**

Our path is not easy, life isn't fair, and things often don't go our way. Disappointment, hardship, and heartache are bound to evoke negative feelings. The book of Psalms encourages you and me to work through those feelings—to get honest with God. But as we spill out our true thoughts and feelings, let's remember not to jettison righteousness and sound doctrine, no matter how unpleasant the road may be. "Faith is the art of holding on to things your reason has once accepted, in spite of your changing moods."[14]

Besides inward focus, Psalms encourages an outward orientation. Many psalms speak of care for others: the poor, foreigners, and those who don't know God. Psalm 40 illustrates the outward-focus principle.

He lifted me out of the slimy pit,
  out of the mud and mire;
he set my feet on a rock
  and gave me a firm place to stand.
He put a new song in my mouth,
  a hymn of praise to our God.
Many will see and fear the LORD
  and put their trust in him. (Psalm 40:2–3)

Because we ourselves have experienced deliverance, we want others to experience it too. We want them to know the same wonderful God we have come to know.

This concern for others should extend well beyond our neighbors. We want the entire world to know God. This flows from a key Old Testament principle: God's plan that all nations be blessed through his people (Genesis 12:3; Exodus 19:6; Isaiah 49:6). Though the seed of this principle will not fully germinate until New Testament times (Matthew 28:19–20; Romans 16:26), it is present embryonically all the same. The shortest Bible chapter (just two chapters before the longest) is clear about this:

Psalm 117

> ¹ *Praise the* LORD*, all you nations;*
> *extol him, all you peoples.*
> ² *For great is his love toward us,*
> *and the faithfulness of the* LORD *endures forever.*
> *Praise the* LORD*.*

The desire to bless others flows naturally from our own experience of salvation. God is saving us not just from hell, but from this world; not just from external harm, but from ourselves. He rescues us from the emptiness and vice of the world. This isn't a one-time event in the past, but an ongoing experience. He rescues us every day! When God touches our hearts and changes our lives like this, we want others to know his mercy too.

Inward orientation and outward orientation: such a double focus is integral to spiritual health. To the extent that the psalms nurture such a genuine spirituality, they have the potential to make us more self-aware, relatable to others, and grounded in God. In short, we become fully human. We move in the direction of Christlikeness. In every sense, we begin to thrive.

Heart questions

- Do I tend to be *excessively* inward-focused? Or *excessively* outward-focused?

- Am I giving sufficient attention to cultivating the inner life?

- What feelings (or subjects or issues) do I have a difficult time expressing to God? Which psalms might help me express myself?

Prayer points

- *"Restore to me the joy of your salvation and grant me a willing spirit, to sustain me. Then I will teach transgressors your ways, so that sinners will turn back to you"* (51:12–13).

- *"He lifted me out of the slimy pit, out of the mud and mire; he set my feet on a rock and gave me a firm place to stand. He put a new song in my mouth, a hymn of praise to our God. Many will see and fear the Lord and put their trust in him"* (40:2–3).

---

[14] C. S. Lewis, *Mere Christianity* (New York: Harper Collins, 2009).

6

THE DARKNESS (PSALMS 12, 46, AND 88)

No one should think that Psalms—or the Bible, for that matter—is a self-improvement plan or an easy road to bliss. (You know the kind of worldly philosophy I'm talking about: "Think the right thoughts, and the world will smile on you.") The Scriptures are profoundly realistic. They acknowledge that the world is often not a happy place. Our own lives may be riddled with pain, injustice, and the confusion arising from both.

Not all is light. Even with sound doctrine, solid faith, and spiritual friends, we may still walk through the Valley of the Shadow of Death.

Through the eyes of faith we recognize that God is in control. Everything that happens is either caused by or permitted by God. That is, ultimately the future rests in his hands. As has been said, "We may not know what the future holds, but we know him who holds the future." And yet it is also equally true that the world is spinning out of control (Psalm 2; 12; 46). The malignant influence of the prince of this world is universal. Evil is not just a theoretical construct.

Psalm 12

[1] *Help, LORD, for no one is faithful anymore;*
those who are loyal have vanished from the human race.
[2] *They lie to their neighbor;*
they flatter with their lips
but harbor deception in their hearts.
[3] *May the LORD silence all flattering lips*
and every boastful tongue—
[4] *those who say,*
"By our tongues we will prevail;
our own lips will defend us—who is lord over us?"
[5] *"Because the poor are plundered and the needy groan,*
I will now arise," says the LORD.
"I will protect them from those who malign them."
[6] *And the words of the LORD are flawless,*
like silver purified in a crucible,
like gold refined seven times.
[7] *You, LORD, will keep the needy safe*
and will protect us forever from the wicked,
[8] *who freely strut about*
when what is vile is honored by the human race.

Ours is a sick world populated by a "corrupt generation" (Acts 2:40). As when Egypt was plagued with a "darkness that [could] be felt" (Exodus 10:21), the world in which we move is flawed, selfishly estranged from God.

Several years ago I was shocked to read about an elderly pig farmer who had gone missing. Eventually they found his dentures—in the pigsty. They were the only part of him the pigs wouldn't eat. Everything else they devoured—flesh, bones, clothes—but not the false teeth. There is truly something dangerous about this dark world. Get too close, and it will consume you.

But the darkness doesn't always come from without. Our own inner darkness is even more palpable, and even more acutely painful.

> **Oh, that my actions would consistently reflect your decrees! Then I will not be ashamed when I compare my life with your commands (Psalm 119:5–6).**

We may be disappointed with our failures to stay on the narrow road—how hard it can be to keep a spiritual focus, to stay righteous no matter what! At other times, we may be regaining spiritual perspective after a time of drought, yet the obstacles to restoration are many. We long for the Holy Spirit to take control of our lives, but still we wake up flat and uninspired. To parrot Persian poet Omar Khayyám, "Indeed, indeed Repentance oft I swore before—but was I sober when I swore?"[15]

Why is it that we're so fickle? We lament, with the psalmist, "Oh, that my actions would consistently reflect your decrees! Then I will not be ashamed when I compare my life with your commands" (Psalm 119:5–6 NLT).

Though we sometimes inflict suffering on ourselves by our own sin, at other times we suffer when we haven't done wrong. We search our hearts and, like Job—someone who could easily have mouthed the words of our next psalm—our conscience is clear in regard to compromise or guilt. Things don't make sense, our theology isn't helping us, and darkness fills the horizon.

Psalms like 44 and 89, which follow the painful psalms 42, 43, and 88, support no easy rationalizations. Things aren't going well, and we can't make sense of our world. Such psalms help us to *live with* theological tensions, as opposed to grabbing at pat explanations for hard things ("She must have been deep in sin if God took her baby"; "If he'd been praying every day, he might not have gotten cancer").

When we insist on having an answer for everything, before thinking things through in light of the full range of Scripture, unreality begins to characterize our faith. People don't relate to us. Our faith-world is too good to be true—because it isn't authentic. Elements of wishful thinking have contaminated the purity of our faith.

Psalm 88

> [1] *LORD, you are the God who saves me;*
>   *day and night I cry out to you.*
> [2] *May my prayer come before you;*
>   *turn your ear to my cry.*
> [3] *I am overwhelmed with troubles*
>   *and my life draws near to death.*

⁴ I am counted among those who go down to the pit;
  I am like one without strength.
⁵ I am set apart with the dead,
  like the slain who lie in the grave,
whom you remember no more,
  who are cut off from your care.
⁶ You have put me in the lowest pit,
  in the darkest depths.
⁷ Your wrath lies heavily on me;
  you have overwhelmed me with all your waves.
⁸ You have taken from me my closest friends
  and have made me repulsive to them.
I am confined and cannot escape;
  ⁹ my eyes are dim with grief.
I call to you, LORD, every day;
  I spread out my hands to you.
¹⁰ Do you show your wonders to the dead?
  Do their spirits rise up and praise you?
¹¹ Is your love declared in the grave,
  your faithfulness in Destruction?
¹² Are your wonders known in the place of darkness,
  or your righteous deeds in the land of oblivion?
¹³ But I cry to you for help, LORD;
  in the morning my prayer comes before you.
¹⁴ Why, LORD, do you reject me

and hide your face from me?
[15] *From my youth I have suffered and been close to death;*
I have borne your terrors and am in despair.
[16] *Your wrath has swept over me;*
your terrors have destroyed me.
[17] *All day long they surround me like a flood;*
they have completely engulfed me.
[18] *You have taken from me friend and neighbor—*
darkness is my closest friend.

In the original Hebrew, the final word of Psalm 88 is "darkness"; a darkness where the writer is *overwhelmed, without strength, grieving, suffering, terrified, engulfed, confused, and lonely.* Pain like this can strangle our hope and stifle our faith.

When my sister died, I felt this darkness in a very palpable way. I entered a phase of both bewilderment and openness to new possibilities. For the previous seven years my relationship with the Lord and his word had been clear. I had moved to Europe on a mission team and was extremely fulfilled in the work of church-building. My friends and I were on the cutting edge in our spiritual walk, constantly growing and inspired as we embraced the challenges of life on the mission field. At that time I had two degrees and was involved in postgraduate theological study in London. The world made sense and life was good! But then, when my sister Suzanne died at age twenty, everything changed.

Her death was unexpected and the shockwave knocked me hard. Suzanne had diabetes, but we had thought it was managed—under control. It wasn't supposed to be fatal. Her loss set me reeling, partly because it was so unexpected, partly because she was gone a few days before I even found out she had passed, and partly because I didn't have anyone to help me through this terribly sad time.

Even though I had experienced the death of someone near to me before (my college roommate was killed just weeks after I became a Christian), losing such a close family member was different. And I had to come to terms with the fact that she was a nonbeliever. Quite understandably, I began to rethink what I really believed about eternal judgment. This opened my mind to other areas as well. I pondered biblical inerrancy. I studied C. S. Lewis on Psalms. I got in touch with the weaknesses of some of the "scientific" arguments buttressing my faith, and began to respect modern biology. (God's book of works—the truths he reveals through the natural world—was not a threat to my faith, but an integral component.) I think I became a more honest person.

Throughout the experience, I had been "disoriented" —that's the word theologians like Walter Brueggemann use to describe the overwhelming, painful darkness that Psalm 88 describes. Brueggemann also suggests that there are psalms of orientation and new orientation in addition to psalms of disorientation.[16]

- *Psalms of Orientation:* These psalms reflect a confident belief that the world is well ordered, reliable, and life-giving to the person of faith. Some examples: 1, 8, 14, 33, 37, 104, 111, 112, 119, 131, 145.

- *Psalms of Disorientation:* These psalms reflect the brokenness of life when it is no longer orderly but savage. Spoken out of the depths, they are still bold acts of faith. Examples: 13, 22, 32, 35, 50, 71, 73, 74, 79, 81, 86, 88, 130, 137, 143.

- *Psalms of New Orientation:* The pit is not the end of life; there is more. New orientation psalms reflect the surprise of new possibilities that are experienced as pure gifts from God. They are full of thanks. Examples: 23, 27, 30, 34, 40, 65, 66, 91, 100, 103, 113, 117, 124, 135, 138, 150.[17]

I didn't recognize the disorientation I experienced as a result of my sister's death until long after. I realized that prior to this event, my relationship with God had been "oriented"; absolute trust and faith in an all-powerful God had been easy. Yet God allowed the disorientation in my life to bring about a new, fuller relationship with him. From that time forward, I was able to be of assistance to many who were facing difficult questions or difficult times. I was still young (twenty-seven), and it was okay that I didn't have all the answers; the journey would last the rest of my life. In short, I was experiencing new orientation. The same God, the same Scriptures—yet a fresh way of relating to them.

Some catalysts of disorientation

- The darkness (sinfulness) of the world (Psalms 12, 14)
- Natural disasters (Psalm 46)
- Betrayal (Psalms 41, 55)
- Deep loneliness (Psalms 25, 88)
- War, displacement, exile (Psalms 74, 126, 137)
- Sickness (Psalms 6, 41)
- The Dark Valley (Psalm 23)
- Continuous and unexplainable trials (Psalms 13, 90)

Fast-forward twenty or thirty years. I came to terms with church problems, family troubles, severe back pain, and of course, many more deaths. This trajectory of reorientation was (and is) continuing. Though I have far to go, the psalms show me it's okay to struggle. God is still at work, even when life is hard or his hand is invisible. I'm sure you've gone through your own tough times—or you will. The psalms can help you through your own darkness, or "winter."

People who write books about the Psalms often cite Brueggemann's classification, above. They are also fond of quoting another theologian, Martin Marty, who speaks of the "wintry landscape of the soul"—which we all become increasingly acquainted with as we age physically and spiritually.

"[Psalm 88] is a scandal to anyone who isolates it from the biblical canon, a pain to anyone who must hear it apart from more lively words. Whoever devises from the Scriptures a philosophy in which everything turns out right has to begin by tearing out this page of the volume."[18]

Disorientation results from myriad causes, and it may be accelerated by the cumulative pressures of life. We will all face times of darkness in our lives—perhaps even an agonizing and numbing "dark night of the soul." The psalms teach us how to acknowledge these feelings, not deny or minimize them. They show us how to *pray through* them—not pray as though everything is fine. For if we ignore our own heart, it's only a matter of time before our faith is damaged.

If you find yourself in a time of darkness, remember this: it's too early to give up hope or to shut down, deciding to feel nothing for fear your honest emotions will overwhelm you. "When dreams shatter and God disappears, we don't need to get mad at Him, to be afraid of Him, or to obey Him from a distance. And we must not resolve to feel nothing deeply. We need rather to realize that He vanishes from our sight to do what He could not do if we could see Him. In the spiritual journey, I know of nothing so difficult to believe. But it's true."[19]

The psalms illustrate how the Lord is at work even in the darkness. God is light and penetrates the darkness of the world (Psalms 27, 105; John 1; 1 John 1). In his own time, he may open the eyes of our heart so that we may see (Ephesians 1:18; John 3:19; Ephesians 6:12; also 2 Kings 6:17).

And yet God's light does more than merely illumine the path, expose sin, or clarify the murky (Psalm 119:105, 90:8; John 3:19; Ephesians 5:13), for eternal light has dawned. In Psalms we find intimations of heaven: 16:11, 17:15 (see Job 19:25–27), 49:15, 73:24.

Even in times of darkness, God points us to hope:

> *The LORD is my light and my salvation—*
> *whom shall I fear?*
> *The LORD is the stronghold of my life—*
> *of whom shall I be afraid?* (Psalm 27:1)

Heart questions

- For me, is the world a dark place? Or am I charmed by it?

- If the earth gave way under my feet, am I confident that I would have God to hold on to?

- Am I allowing his light to illuminate my life? Do I realize that he offers light through every book in Scripture?

- Do I appreciate the value of honesty about my own fears, doubts, and pain—how this lends an air of genuineness and hope to my outreach, fellowship, and counseling?

- Does the darkness of this world cause me to yearn for God's new world? And yet the new creation has already begun (2 Corinthians 5:17). Do I grasp this?

Prayer points

- Shine your light into the dark places of my life.

- Help me to be more honest and open about my own fears and disorientation.

- Help me to see every intimation of the next world in the Scriptures, and find comfort in it.

[15] *The Rubáiyát of Omar Khayyám*, 94. Kyayyám lived from AD 1048 to 1131.

[16] Walter Brueggemann, *Praying the Psalms: Engaging Scripture and the Life of the Spirit* (Eugene, OR: Cascade, 2007).

[17] These explanations and examples have been excerpted from Fr. William Parker, "Psalms of Orientation, Disorientation, and New Orientation," www.ascensioncatholic.net/TOPICS/bible/Psalms.html.

[18] Martin Marty, *A Cry of Absence: Reflections for the Winter of the Heart* (San Francisco: Harper & Row, 1983), 68.

[19] Larry Crabb, *Shattered Dreams: God's Unexpected Pathway to Joy* (Colorado Springs: WaterBrook Press, 2001), 158.

7
WHEN I'M DRIFTING (PSALMS 73 AND 37)

The psalms portray trials in multiple ways. Sometimes trials feel like drowning (18:16; 32:6; 69:1–2, 14; 124:3–5). In Psalm 69, the waters have surged up to the writer's neck. Flailing, he can barely take in a breath. Hard times may fall upon us suddenly, dragging us out to sea like a terrifying rip current. In other metaphors for times of difficulty, we slip (Psalm 17:5; 18:36; 37:31; 66:9; 73:2, 18; 94:18). We fall (38:17, 56:13, 118:13, 145:14). We're attacked by wild beasts (22:12–16, 57:4, 74:19). We lose our memory (59:11, 78:7).

Despite the torrent of vivid metaphors, more often than not spiritual deterioration is less dramatic. Like dim-witted sheep (119:176), we simply wander off. Hebrews 2:1 urges, "We must pay the most careful attention, therefore, to what we have heard, so that we do not drift away." The word "drift" is a nautical term, as when a boat has not been properly moored. When we neglect God's word, it's easy to drift.

Once adrift, our outside may cease to match our inside. Proverbs 5:14 tells us that we can be at the brink of ruin, even when we are surrounded by God's people ("the assembly").

Even though we attend the assembly (which is the translation of "church"), we can still be in a bad place spiritually. We may feel like outsiders.

There are times when we all feel separated, lonely. I will always remember one nighttime meeting, when I was only a few weeks old in Christ. My fellow college students from Duke and UNC were informally talking in twos. For the moment, I found myself the odd man out among my new friends, so I walked outside for a breath of fresh air. From a nearby hill, I stared at the group through the window. To me the Christians, paired in conversation, looked like mannequins. I suddenly felt like an outsider.

An eerie wave of doubt washed over me. Was my new faith real? Did I belong with these believers? I recognized the feeling—from before I was a Christian. After a few minutes, I gingerly decided to go back inside, to (literally) be an insider once more. Only then did my doubts and fears fade. Sometimes we need to make decisions like that—to return to the fellowship and get involved—especially when our feelings fluctuate, or we don't feel 100 percent, or maybe when the church is less than attractive. (Let's be honest: Sometimes church can be dull, or even embarrassing.)

When we drift emotionally, we don't feel connected. It doesn't take much for us to end up in some scary places. We're attracted to the world and its idols: financial security, reputation, fashion, food, comfort and pleasures, "stuff"— everything the world has to offer (1 John 2:15–17). We become good at rationalizing our sin, our materialism (Luke 8:14;

Revelation 3:14–18). We don't seek out the counsel of spiritual persons or imitate their consistency (Hebrews 6:12; 13:7).

The psalms we'll survey in this chapter are 73 and 37. Both contain warnings and encouragements, and they connect nicely with one another. I think you'll discover, as I have, that they will help you not to drift. And if you do drift, they will help you to anchor again.

Psalm 73

[1] Surely God is good to Israel,
to those who are pure in heart.
[2] But as for me, my feet had almost slipped;
I had nearly lost my foothold.
[3] For I envied the arrogant
when I saw the prosperity of the wicked.
[4] They have no struggles;
their bodies are healthy and strong.
[5] They are free from common human burdens;
they are not plagued by human ills.
[6] Therefore pride is their necklace;
they clothe themselves with violence.
[7] From their callous hearts comes iniquity;
their evil imaginations have no limits.
[8] They scoff, and speak with malice;
with arrogance they threaten oppression.
[9] Their mouths lay claim to heaven,
and their tongues take possession of the earth.

¹⁰ *Therefore their people turn to them*
and drink up waters in abundance.
¹¹ *They say, "How would God know?*
Does the Most High know anything?"
¹² *This is what the wicked are like—*
always free of care, they go on amassing wealth.
¹³ *Surely in vain I have kept my heart pure*
and have washed my hands in innocence.
¹⁴ *All day long I have been afflicted,*
and every morning brings new punishments.
¹⁵ *If I had spoken out like that,*
I would have betrayed your children.
¹⁶ *When I tried to understand all this,*
it troubled me deeply
¹⁷ *till I entered the sanctuary of God;*
then I understood their final destiny.
¹⁸ *Surely you place them on slippery ground;*
you cast them down to ruin.
¹⁹ *How suddenly are they destroyed,*
completely swept away by terrors!
²⁰ *They are like a dream when one awakes;*
when you arise, LORD,
you will despise them as fantasies.
²¹ *When my heart was grieved*
and my spirit embittered,
²² *I was senseless and ignorant;*
I was a brute beast before you.

²³ Yet I am always with you;
you hold me by my right hand.
²⁴ You guide me with your counsel,
and afterward you will take me into glory.
²⁵ Whom have I in heaven but you?
And earth has nothing I desire besides you.
²⁶ My flesh and my heart may fail,
but God is the strength of my heart
and my portion forever.
²⁷ Those who are far from you will perish;
you destroy all who are unfaithful to you.
²⁸ But as for me, it is good to be near God.
I have made the Sovereign LORD my refuge;
I will tell of all your deeds.

The psalmist had almost slipped (v2) when he began to envy those who did not honor God (v3; see Ecclesiastes 4:4). It seemed as though *they* were receiving God's blessing. It wasn't fair! A friend of mine once told me about attending a huge wedding. Seven hundred smiling guests were treated to a steak and lobster dinner. Everyone was so pleasant. My friend admitted that as he looked around at the signs of wealth and earthly happiness, he felt pulled. He wanted to believe this large crowd of polite, respectable persons was all right—that perhaps they didn't need God. Like the prosperous individuals of Psalm 73, their enviable lifestyles made the person of faith question his efforts to live righteously.

Some of us who have chosen the path of Christian ministry live with the knowledge that we might have made double our present income—if only we'd chosen a different field. Sometimes that knowledge is frustrating.

Everyone wants the good life. This temptation can even affect entire churches, some of which offer their prospective members a "church home" where they are accepted as they are and never called higher. Why would the preacher risk losing members by making them uncomfortable? These churches often preach an attractive message of prosperity—particularly in connection with donations to the church. How are these affluent congregations really that different from the world? Their values seem identical.

The wicked in Psalm 73 weren't necessarily anti-religion, but to them God was unreal. His existence and authority made no difference in their lives (v11). While they went free and unpunished, the psalmist suffered. Devotion to the Lord felt futile (v13). Yet, just in time, the psalmist caught himself (v15). He continued to be deeply troubled (v16) until he entered the sanctuary of God (v17). Was this a high-impact visit to the Jerusalem temple, or a normal visit? Either way, and in the light of eternity, he came to understand their final destiny (vv17–20, 27).

His envy had not been well grounded—and neither is ours. The gospel of health and wealth ("peace, peace"—Jeremiah 6:14) is hollow. The true gospel is a call to holiness. As for the greater income many ministers might have had with a "secular" job, the extra wealth could easily have numbed their souls to the things of God. And as for the seven-hundred-guest wedding, my friend later told me that, sadly, the couple divorced within a few years. The hollowness of the world may not always be exposed immediately—or even in this life—but it certainly will be in the next. We must hold on to an eternal perspective.

"When my heart was grieved and my spirit embittered I was senseless and ignorant; I was a brute beast before you" (vv21–22). In other words, without a spiritual outlook, we're on the same level as the animals. When we envy the world, we behave like the world and take what we can. But when we give our heart to God, we bask in his presence—a prelude to eternal glory (vv23–24). There's no need to worry about money, financial security, or impressing the neighbors. Our inheritance, or portion, is the Lord himself (v26).

Summing up Psalm 73, we see that we can begin to slip away when we overly admire the lives of those who aren't putting the Lord first. These people aren't necessarily opposed to religion; they just don't comprehend why God would care about their behavior. We too may begin to feel that faith is futile. It's not getting us anywhere—certainly not by worldly standards. If we give in to this way of thinking, before we realize it, we will drift to a dangerous place. Fortunately, rescue from such a perilous trajectory comes once we enter the sanctuary of God. "Better is one day in your courts than a thousand elsewhere; I would rather be a doorkeeper in the house of my God than dwell in the tents of the wicked" (Psalm 84:10).

> **We can slip away when we overly admire the lives of those not putting the Lord first.**

Only from the vantage point of holiness, from a spiritual perspective, can we appreciate the final destiny of those who are outsiders to the Lord. Sooner or later their bubble will burst. Without such a perspective, we resemble the animals, not giving a thought to our Creator. Fortunately, the psalmist regained his perspective: an eternal one. At the end of the psalm, now realigned and rebalanced, he feels confident to stand up for God, to "tell of… [his] deeds." When the Lord and the spiritual world are real to us, we naturally begin to speak about them to others.

Psalm 37 contains similar thoughts. It urges us not to fret and assures us that it is the meek who will inherit the earth—not the powerful.

Psalm 37

> [1] *Do not fret because of those who are evil*
>   *or be envious of those who do wrong;*
> [2] *for like the grass they will soon wither,*
>   *like green plants they will soon die away.*
> [3] *Trust in the LORD and do good;*
>   *dwell in the land and enjoy safe pasture.*

⁴ Take delight in the LORD,
and he will give you the desires of your heart.
⁵ Commit your way to the LORD;
trust in him and he will do this:
⁶ He will make your righteous reward shine like the dawn,
your vindication like the noonday sun.
⁷ Be still before the LORD
and wait patiently for him;
do not fret when people succeed in their ways,
when they carry out their wicked schemes.
⁸ Refrain from anger and turn from wrath;
do not fret—it leads only to evil.
⁹ For those who are evil will be destroyed,
but those who hope in the LORD will inherit the land…

²³ The LORD makes firm the steps
of the one who delights in him;
²⁴ though he may stumble, he will not fall,
for the LORD upholds him with his hand.
²⁵ I was young and now I am old,
yet I have never seen the righteous forsaken
or their children begging bread.
²⁶ They are always generous and lend freely;
their children will be a blessing.
²⁷ Turn from evil and do good;
then you will dwell in the land forever.
²⁸ For the LORD loves the just

and will not forsake his faithful ones.
Wrongdoers will be completely destroyed;
*   the offspring of the wicked will perish.*
²⁹ The righteous will inherit the land
*   and dwell in it forever.*
³⁰ The mouths of the righteous utter wisdom,
*   and their tongues speak what is just.*
³¹ The law of their God is in their hearts;
*   their feet do not slip.*

Drifting may originate in envy, leading to false comparisons and fretting (vv1, 7, 8; see also Proverbs 24:19). We fret over finances. We fret about health matters. We fret over the apparent prosperity of nonbelievers, and we may even fret as we compare ourselves to brothers or sisters in Christ.

Yet fretting is unproductive. The psalms teach us: Don't worry about the next fellow; work on your own life. Delight yourself in the Lord. Focus! (vv3–6). Ensure that God's word is filling your heart (v31). (Recall the crucial lessons from our study of Psalms 19 and 119.)

Do you get yourself worked up? Do things eat at you, eroding your joy and distorting your spiritual vision? The Lord knows how we are tempted to be anxious. Jesus was tempted in all the ways that we are (Hebrews 2:18, 4:15). Yet too often we think like Peter, who wrongly compared himself to another disciple of Jesus. Peter apparently thought it unfair that the other fellow might live into old age, while he was destined for martyrdom (John 21:18–19). Peter was needlessly fretting.

> *When Peter saw him, he asked, "Lord, what about him?"*
>
> *Jesus answered, "If I want him to remain alive until I return, what is that to you? You must follow me."* (John 21:21–22)

Peter's attitude is understandable, but misdirected. It is in following Jesus that we find our meaning and true purpose. We don't need to worry about others. The Lord will take care of them (Romans 14:4).

The take-away

When we read psalms like 73 and 37, we realize that God knows us intimately, including the temptations and distractions that derail us from following him. He knows when we are drifting, and in his grace, he provides a way to get back on course.

The psalms are extremely diverse and address many of our emotional and spiritual needs. In many of the psalms—up to forty percent of which entail grief, sadness, or regret—the psalmist finds resolution by the end of the prayer. Do you want to grow more mature in the Lord? Let him help you! Pray through the troubles and dive into his word, which contains the wise counsel we need.

At one time or another we will relate to the entire range of psalms. Be sure to take a peek at the table "Psalms for Every Occasion" at the end of this book. With 150 sacred psalms in the canon, the Lord has anticipated all our needs. Naturally, a passage that speaks to one person may not be relevant to another (at least not yet). Some passages take on fresh meaning as we age or face fresh challenges.

All of this means that we need to learn to use the psalms to minister to ourselves. I have my favorites. For example, Psalm 37 calms my heart when I'm anxious. Psalm 48 gives me perspective; it has been especially meaningful since I walked around the walls of Jerusalem, contemplating the kingdom of God. I love Psalm 49, which speaks about true wealth, and Psalm 50, on true religion. Have you ever had a dry spell? Psalm 63 is great for those who, like David, are in the wilderness.

> **We need to learn to use the psalms to minister to ourselves.**

Those are some of my favorites; look into your heart, search the Scriptures, and find *your* psalms. Anchoring scriptures can make a huge difference in our perspective, in how we feel. Determine to become a more faithful student of the Bible. Hold on to his word and let it minister to your heart as God intended.

And if you've drifted, don't worry, but put your trust in the Lord. "O Lord Almighty, blessed is the man who trusts in you" (Psalm 84:12; also Psalm 32:10). As someone said, "If God seems far away, guess who moved?" He *always* longs for our fellowship to be restored (Psalm 23; Revelation 3:19–20). Come back to the course God has charted for you. Let his word guide you back and anchor you.

Heart questions

- When was the last time I was drifting? How did I lose my moorings?
- Which psalms and other scriptures keep me anchored to the Lord and prevent me from drifting?
- Do I have an eternal perspective on this world? Do I see the people of this world in perspective, as mere humans?
- Can I locate any more points of contact between Psalms 37 and 73?
- How might I benefit from working through my feelings/issues in prayer?

Prayer points

- Lord, keep me from drifting.
- When I find that I am drifting, help me to come back.
- And then prevent me from ever slipping away again.

8
CREATE IN ME A PURE HEART (PSALM 51)

In this chapter we come to one of the "penitential psalms" (6, 32, 38, 51, 102, 130, and 143). The oft-quoted fifty-first is nearly as famous as the beloved twenty-third. Both mention restoration of the soul, though in the case of Psalm 51, the theme governs the entire work.

When I was baptized into Christ, I felt God's cleansing. Soon afterward, in the North Carolina woods, I attended a college retreat based on Psalm 51. Each lesson took its title from one of the psalm's verses, and I remember those lessons to this day. I was on fire for God. I didn't need to be restored—not *then*, anyway.

Few things will help us to get back on track with God faster than longing for a pure heart (Matthew 5:8). Of course, there's no benefit if we're keeping secrets, holding on to unconfessed sin, or pretending to be more "together" than we really are. But when we hit rock bottom, when we're sick and tired of being sick and tired and we care more about the truth than about our pride, this psalm can work wonders.

Psalm 51 is coupled with the account of David and Bathsheba (2 Samuel 11–12), a story of sin, cover-up, confession, and restoration. Since we're all subject to moral drift (to put it nicely), the psalm speaks just as loudly to us today as it did during the second millennium before Christ. Let's unpack David's humble, emotional, and genuine appeal for mercy.

His sin has been exposed by a true prophet and true friend, Nathan. With this prompting—and few of us are likely to turn ourselves in without some help from our friends!—David repents, accepts divine discipline, and prepares to move forward. If only every Christ-follower would *get up* after a fall, instead of just lying there (Jeremiah 8:4)!

Keep in mind the framework of *orientation-disorientation-new orientation*. It could be assumed that after the disastrous marital affair, David and his family would be forevermore disoriented. Yet in terms of his walk with God, David kept growing into a man after God's own heart (1 Samuel 13:14, before the affair; 2 Samuel 16:11–12, 21:1, 22:1–51, 23:2–5, after the affair; and Acts 13:22, describing him many generations later).

Psalm 51

> [1] *Have mercy on me, O God,*
> *according to your unfailing love;*
> *according to your great compassion*
> *blot out my transgressions.*
> [2] *Wash away all my iniquity*
> *and cleanse me from my sin.*

³ For I know my transgressions,
    and my sin is always before me.
⁴ Against you, you only, have I sinned
    and done what is evil in your sight;
so you are right in your verdict
    and justified when you judge.
⁵ Surely I was sinful at birth,
    sinful from the time my mother conceived me.

The psalmist pleads for mercy. In the Old Testament sacrificial system, all sins could be blotted out except murder and rape. If David was guilty of these sins—abusing his royal power to force himself on Bathsheba (could she have said no to the king?), and then ordering the death of her husband—then all he could do would be to throw himself on the mercy of the Judge.[20]

Because our sin ultimately strikes against God (v4; Genesis 39:9; 2 Samuel 12:9–10, 13; Proverbs 14:31, 17:5), our uncleanness is *actual*, not merely psychological. This means we can't restore ourselves; only God can do this for us.

Sin isn't washed away by the passage of time. Time may afford a broader perspective, but it doesn't heal. Whoever claimed "time heals all" was dead wrong. Time may bury sin, but if sin isn't confessed, the sinner can never be right with God, nor be whole (Leviticus 5:5; Numbers 5:5–7). And the Lord cannot be fooled, because he looks into the heart of every man and is not deceived by false humility or motives (1 Chronicles 28:9).

Many prayers for forgiveness were uttered in the ancient world, but not at the humility level of the fifty-first psalm. For example, the Hittites "attempted to sway the gods in their direction by averring innocence on the basis of ignorance, by citing the frailty of human beings, by noting their faithfulness to the gods, and by promising praise and sacrifice if their prayers were answered."[21]

Not so David. He made no excuses. He was forgiven (2 Samuel 12:13), but still there were consequences. "David had infected all his children with the sins of violence and lust"[22] for generations to come, just as the Father told his people in Exodus 20:5. Sin always has consequences.

A comment is in order about v5. This is *not* support for the early medieval doctrine of original sin.[23] Compare Psalms 71:6, 22:9, and 58:3—the psalmist did not mean his words literally, any more than Paul did in 1 Timothy 1:15. Considering how much Paul had been given (and forgiven), he may have been more aware of his shortcomings than others, yet surely the Lord would not have us rank Paul as more immoral than Genghis Khan or Joseph Stalin! But that's the point: It's about how we perceive ourselves, not where we fall in the sin rankings.

"Sinful at birth" is nothing more than the projection of a present *feeling* of sinfulness back to the earliest possible point in the psalmist's life. We have a proclivity towards selfishness (Genesis 8:21)—for biological and psychological reasons— yet God calls us to act beyond the level of mere self-interest

(Philippians 2:3–4). We are to rise above the level of the flesh (our animal nature) to the realm of the spirit.

Sins from which our generation has special need of forgiveness include arrogance, materialism and consumerism, lust and Internet pornography, and ingratitude and entitlement. How do I know? Not only have I seen their pervasive effects on the culture and people around me, but I myself have been guilty of all of these. And so, in humility I should probably confess not, "I *have* sinned," but rather, "I *am* a sinner." These sins run deep. Yet through Christ I have overcome—and so can we all. God makes us whiter than snow (v7). And out of appreciation, we forgive others.

These verses are rich.[24] Perhaps our true understanding of them is best confirmed not by an essay, but by our interactions. "Blessed are the merciful" (Matthew 5:7, as in 18:21–35). Am I merciful towards others (Ephesians 4:32; Colossians 3:13)?

6 Yet you desired faithfulness even in the womb;
  you taught me wisdom in that secret place.
7 Cleanse me with hyssop, and I will be clean;
  wash me, and I will be whiter than snow.
8 Let me hear joy and gladness;
  let the bones you have crushed rejoice.
9 Hide your face from my sins
  and blot out all my iniquity.
10 Create in me a pure heart, O God,

and renew a steadfast spirit within me.
11 Do not cast me from your presence
*   or take your Holy Spirit from me.*
12 Restore to me the joy of your salvation
*   and grant me a willing spirit, to sustain me.*

Hyssop was used for cleansing in Levitical ceremonies, for cleansing from leprosy, or for contact with death (Exodus 12; Leviticus 14; Numbers 19). Interestingly, hyssop contains thymol, a disinfectant. Verse 8 recalls Proverbs 17:22. In vv9–10, David isn't asking to be let off. He's asking for transformation—a new spirit, a common longing in the prophetic literature, such as in Isaiah and Ezekiel.

The phrase "Holy Spirit" in v11 (or holy spirit—there are no capital letters in Hebrew) is rare in the Old Testament. The phrase appears only here and in Isaiah 63:10–11. If God is spirit, then he is present in Spirit. This is probably not an instance of indwelling, as the Spirit was not given in this way before Jesus' ascension (John 7:39; Acts 2:30, 33). Here the verse is referencing either the presence of God or perhaps a spirit that is holy.

The joy of our salvation (v12) is more than a feeling. It entails willingness. God will not force us. In a sense, the psalmist is asking God for a holy spirit—to make him holy through and through. We too should pray for this spirit. Jesus says the Father will give the Holy Spirit to those who ask him (Luke 11:13). Holiness and integrity are required if we are to enter God's presence and dwell there (Psalm 15).

[13] *Then I will teach transgressors your ways,*
  so that sinners will turn back to you.
[14] *Deliver me from the guilt of bloodshed, O God,*
  you who are God my Savior,
  and my tongue will sing of your righteousness.
[15] *Open my lips, LORD,*
  and my mouth will declare your praise.
[16] *You do not delight in sacrifice, or I would bring it;*
  you do not take pleasure in burnt offerings.
[17] *My sacrifice, O God, is a broken spirit;*
  a broken and contrite heart
  you, God, will not despise.

We can't keep the good news to ourselves (v13). It's hard to stay motivated in evangelism when all we seek are results or recognition. But it's easy to keep going when we maintain a constant awareness of who we are (God's children in Christ) and when gratitude is continually welling up from our inmost being! Further, the good news isn't a message of self-help. It's a return to God, whether in initial conversion or at any time subsequently.

Verse 14 shows us that guilt is a reality, not just a feeling. Psychologists and psychiatrists lacking a biblical orientation may miss this. True healing (therapy) requires acknowledgement of guilt and taking ownership (Proverbs 30:20). "Guilt of bloodshed" is a phrase often occurring in the context of murder. Worship is the natural response to the experience of cleansing, and results from gratitude to God for his mercy and grace.

This psalm illustrates how religion without heart is worthless (vv15–16; also Psalms 50 and 15). Jesus preached the same in Mark 7. This is not to say that we can dispense with formal faith. The last verse of the psalm doesn't dismiss the sacrificial system—which would be replaced only after the death, resurrection, and ascension of Christ. Notice again the strong emphasis on the heart in v17. See also Psalm 34:18.

Psalm 51 ends here. You may be saying, "Hold on, Douglas. What about the final two verses?"

> [18] *May it please you to prosper Zion,*
> *to build up the walls of Jerusalem.*
> [19] *Then you will delight in the sacrifices of the righteous,*
> *in burnt offerings offered whole;*
> *then bulls will be offered on your altar.*

Many of the psalms show signs of editing. It is difficult to conceive of someone living in the tenth century BC (David) longing for the day when the walls of Jerusalem will be *rebuilt* and animal sacrifices *resumed*. The new ending of the psalm, updating it and making it meaningful and more applicable to God's people in exile, indicates a date after the fall of Jerusalem to the Babylonians (587 BC). It probably originates from the time of Ezra and Nehemiah. The psalm is thus exilic or postexilic—at least in its final form.[25]

Of course whether or not David is the author of the final

verses is immaterial. This beautiful psalm of repentance and redemption speaks to us all. At various points in our lives, we will find ourselves in the position of begging for cleansing and a new beginning, in the presence of a holy and merciful God.

Now that you've finished this chapter, it might be fruitful to read aloud (or pray) the entire psalm once more, to cement into place any insights you've gained. For thousands of years, God-fearing people have borrowed these words from the man after God's own heart to help them draw near to God in times of spiritual crisis. Make David's prayer your own, and watch what happens in your heart as you open yourself up to God's cleansing. Return to this prayer again and again— whenever you need restoration and renewal in your inmost being.

Heart questions

- It has been said that we aren't sinners because we sin (a mere definition), but that we sin because we are sinners (our condition). Do I agree with this?

- Do I get offended if others point out to me the very sins that I should be confessing to God anyway? How deep does my humility go? Do I accept the depth of my sinfulness as David did?

- Am I the sort of person who strives to "self-restore," or do I let others into my life?

- When did I last experience such tangible joy in my salvation that I *had* to express it, whether in words of praise in worship, or in outreach through evangelism?

Prayer points

- My sin is profound, and I offer no excuses. Have mercy on me. I long for the cleansing only you can give.

- May joy in your salvation accompany me as I follow you daily, and may others sense your presence in my life.

- Keep my heart in a broken, contrite, moldable, honest, and teachable condition. I long for consistency!

- As you continually restore me, O Lord, may I continue to seek to restore others.

---

[20] C. S. Lewis, *Reflections on the Psalms,* 12. Actually, the scene is even more Christian than Jewish. As C. S. Lewis and others noted, when the ancient Jews came to God, they asked for justice (as if they were plaintiffs in a civil case); when Christians come, they ask for mercy (as though they are defendants in a criminal case). The former come to God with conviction that they are in the right; the latter too often come to the Lord in fear of rejection.

[21] Kenton L. Sparks, *Ancient Texts for the Study of the Hebrew Bible: A Guide to the Background Literature* (Peabody, Mass: Hendrickson, 2005), 112.

[22] George A. F. Knight, *The Daily Bible Study Series, Psalms Vol. I*, 243.

[23] The commonly cited Romans 5:12 cannot support the doctrine, for if it did, then Romans 5:19 would mean that all humans will be saved, even against their will. See http://www.douglasjacoby.com/originalsinmp3/.

[24] Much more emerges from these verses. Three examples must suffice. In vv1–2 there are three verbs for forgiveness, just as in vv3–4 there are three different words for sin. Consult a Bible dictionary to probe the nuances. Second, consider the structure of Psalm 51:1:

> *Have mercy on me, O God,*
>   *according to your unfailing love;*
>   *according to your great compassion*
>   *blot out my transgressions.*

In most Hebrew poetry we find "thought-rhyme," as opposed to sound rhyme, the mark of most Western poetry. The second line in the couplet parallels and expounds on the first (have mercy/blot out). Finally, students of literature will also notice the chiasm, or ABBA arrangement (have mercy/love/compassion/blot out).

[25] Knight, 247. The commentator takes vv15–19 as a two-stage extension of David's original psalm.

9

PRAYERS YOU SHOULDN'T PRAY
(PSALMS 139, 137, 58, AND 109)

Emulating the prayer—and *pray-er* of Psalm 51, with his heartfelt confession—is healthy for relationships, especially for our most vital relationship of all. Yet although truthfulness is commendable, Psalms contains some prayers that are *sub-Christian* in content and attitude. They are honest, but not gracious. On the one hand, they are part of Scripture, and God wills that we learn from them. On the other hand, there are aspects we as Christians are bound to reject. Hence our chapter, "Prayers You Shouldn't Pray."

We are often oblivious to our own heart, unaware of its contradictions. In a previous chapter we highlighted the final verses of Psalm 139, a psalm cherished by Bible readers the world over. But might we be reading selectively? For backing up a little in this psalm, we read:

> *¹⁹ Oh that you would slay the wicked, O God!*
> *O men of blood, depart from me!*
> *²⁰ They speak against you with malicious intent;*
> *your enemies take your name in vain.*

> [21] *Do I not hate those who hate you, O LORD?*
>   *And do I not loathe those who rise up against you?*
> [22] *I hate them with complete hatred;*
>   *I count them my enemies.*
> [23] *Search me, O God, and know my heart!*
>   *Try me and know my thoughts!*
> [24] *And see if there be any grievous way in me,*
>   *and lead me in the way everlasting!* ESV

In the same breath the psalmist both curses his enemies and asks the Lord to see if there is any grievous (or "offensive" in the NIV) way in him. By God's righteous standards, he has just testified against himself! What are we to make of this?

The psalms originate in the period of the old covenant. They were written long before God visited our planet in Jesus Christ and fully revealed his holy standards. The "rules" changed with the new covenant. Jesus raised the bar. No longer are we permitted to curse, hate, or kill (Matthew 5:21–26, 38–48). Since this part of the Lord's will hadn't been revealed in the time of Psalm 139, it would be unfair of us to hold the psalmist to the Christian standard.

With this in mind, let's examine three of the "imprecatory psalms." The term comes from Latin. Literally, it means praying against (one's enemies), from *prex* (prayer) + *in* (against). There are many such prayers in the Old Testament, not only in Psalms.

Psalm 137

[1] *By the rivers of Babylon we sat and wept*
   when we remembered Zion.

[2] *There on the poplars*
   we hung our harps,

[3] *for there our captors asked us for songs,*
   our tormentors demanded songs of joy;
   they said, "Sing us one of the songs of Zion!"

[4] *How can we sing the songs of the LORD*
   while in a foreign land?

[5] *If I forget you, Jerusalem,*
   may my right hand forget its skill.

[6] *May my tongue cling to the roof of my mouth*
   if I do not remember you,

if I do not consider Jerusalem
   my highest joy.

[7] *Remember, LORD, what the Edomites did*
   on the day Jerusalem fell.

"Tear it down," they cried,
   "tear it down to its foundations!"

[8] *Daughter Babylon, doomed to destruction,*
   happy is the one who repays you
   according to what you have done to us.

[9] *Happy is the one who seizes your infants*
   and dashes them against the rocks.

The setting of Psalm 137 is the fall of Jerusalem at the hand of the Babylonians, egged on by the neighboring

Edomites (587 BC). From exile in Babylon an ancient Jew poured forth these heart-wrenching words. Verses 5 and 6 are recited by Jewish grooms as they break a glass by stomping on it as part of the marriage ceremony, to signify that even at a time of "highest joy," a glass is destroyed in order to remember the destruction of the Temple.

The tone changes from longing for Jerusalem to vindictiveness (vv7–9). Since the Babylonians killed many Israelite babies—preventing the children from growing up to take revenge?—responding in kind would have been expected (see Judges 15:11).

Psalm 58

¹ Do you rulers indeed speak justly?
  Do you judge people with equity?
² No, in your heart you devise injustice,
  and your hands mete out violence on the earth...

⁶ Break the teeth in their mouths, O God;
  LORD, tear out the fangs of those lions!
⁷ Let them vanish like water that flows away;
  when they draw the bow, let their arrows fall short.
⁸ May they be like a slug that melts away as it moves along,
  like a stillborn child that never sees the sun.
⁹ Before your pots can feel the heat of the thorns—
  whether they be green or dry—the wicked will be swept
  away.

¹⁰ The righteous will be glad when they are avenged,
when they dip their feet in the blood of the wicked.
¹¹ Then people will say,
"Surely the righteous still are rewarded;
surely there is a God who judges the earth."

Here God's people dream of bathing their feet in the blood of their enemies, who are ruling over them in a harsh and ungodly manner. There is no evidence that the vengeance longed for in any of these three psalms was actually ever carried out. Perhaps they took comfort in mere contemplation of the undoing of the wicked.

Psalm 109

¹ My God, whom I praise,
do not remain silent,
² for people who are wicked and deceitful
have opened their mouths against me;
they have spoken against me with lying tongues.
³ With words of hatred they surround me;
they attack me without cause.
⁴ In return for my friendship they accuse me,
but I am a man of prayer.
⁵ They repay me evil for good,
and hatred for my friendship.
⁶ Appoint someone evil to oppose my enemy;
let an accuser stand at his right hand.

7 *When he is tried, let him be found guilty,*
   and may his prayers condemn him.
8 *May his days be few;*
   may another take his place of leadership.
9 *May his children be fatherless*
   and his wife a widow.
10 *May his children be wandering beggars;*
   may they be driven from their ruined homes.
11 *May a creditor seize all he has;*
   may strangers plunder the fruits of his labor.
12 *May no one extend kindness to him*
   or take pity on his fatherless children.
13 *May his descendants be cut off,*
   their names blotted out from the next generation…

26 *Help me, LORD my God;*
   save me according to your unfailing love.
27 *Let them know that it is your hand,*
   that you, LORD, have done it.
28 *While they curse, may you bless;*
   may those who attack me be put to shame,
   but may your servant rejoice.
29 *May my accusers be clothed with disgrace*
   and wrapped in shame as in a cloak.

In our final selection, at first we are led to believe the psalmist, though unfairly accused, will occupy the moral high ground. He is, after all, a man of prayer (v4). Yet he wishes evil on not only his betrayer, but on his entire family—not unlike the final verse of Psalm 137. In an even more jarring inconsistency of character, the psalmist considers himself a man of prayer, and views prospective vengeance as a sign of God's unfailing love! Nor is this the only psalm where such "unchristian" thoughts occur (31:6). In Psalms 5:5 and 11:5, *God* is said to hate the wicked. (And see Ezekiel 18:23, 32— God takes no pleasure in the death of anyone!) It is doubtful that many Christians will be able to agree with these words— we understand that their inclusion in the Bible does not mean they convey the truth about our God.

It will serve us well to remember that these are *human* words, functioning in a certain way in God's word. Unlike the Torah or the Epistles, most of the psalms are human words directed to God, not God's words directed towards humans, except in that God saw fit to include such words in the biblical canon. (Just as he includes the words of Satan and many enemies of his purposes.)

The Old Testament and enemies

Are we to conclude that under the old covenant, the people of faith had no inkling of the Lord's ultimate peaceful purpose—that they were incurably violent or beholden to their culture without hope of improvement?

The imprecatory psalms exist in tension with the biblical ideal of treating one's enemies well (Exodus 23:4–5; Leviticus 19:17–18; Proverbs 24:17, 25:21; 2 Kings 6:20–23).

Now, the Old Testament may seem to say more about war than about peace, yet peace was always the ultimate and universal goal.[26] The messianic age was to be a time of peace (Isaiah 9:6, 11:6–9).

Zechariah 14:16 is but one of many passages where those traditionally viewed as Israel's enemies are envisioned as spiritual equals, converting to Judaism and sharing in the promises Yahweh made to his people: "Then the survivors from all the nations that have attacked Jerusalem will go up year after year to worship the King, the Lord Almighty, and to celebrate the Feast of Tabernacles." (See also Psalm 117.)

However one understands the difficult passages of the first testament, it is beyond dispute that as Christians we are called to a higher standard (Matthew 5:43–48). For people under the old covenant, it was completely normal to be kind to the insider, while the outsider (non-Israelite) was viewed as the other, the enemy. But do Christians even have enemies? In fact, while the Torah may occasionally have required "no mercy" (Deuteronomy 7:2), in the New Testament we are warned by James, in the spirit of his brother Jesus, that judgment without mercy will be shown to us if we are not merciful (James 2:13). This warning reflects Jesus' teaching about the brotherhood of man. We may not be brothers in the sense of salvation, but we are in the sense of origin. God is the Father of us all, if not in the salvific sense, at least in the ultimate sense.

We *could* utter imprecatory prayers. The question is: Should we? Would it be therapeutic? The world speaks of "sweet revenge." God's word reveals, especially in the New Testament, that a vengeful spirit does not please him. Honest prayers, yes! Get it out. But revenge—no. We must let the Spirit of Christ guide our thoughts and help us find a righteous attitude, even as we pour out to God the hurt and anger we sometimes confront within our own hearts.

Christians, who say they value truth and will follow it wherever it leads, must be honest interpreters of Scripture. That means admitting, even to our critics, that there are "problem passages" in the Bible—passages like these that make people look twice and wonder if God is contradicting himself. Really, such texts should bother us more than outsiders, since they potentially cast aspersions on the God we serve. It's not easy to be so open, so honest. When you've based your life on the trustworthiness of the Scriptures, it takes great courage to admit that there are difficulties. But we can't just shrug our shoulders and say, "Oh, well, I don't know what to do with that scripture. I believe anyway." If we are going to be students of the Bible who are equipped to help others with the difficult questions of faith, we must study and think and work through these questions ourselves—we won't always find easy answers, but we can usually find resolution that honors God and is faithful to his character and his word.

Back to the point: Jesus called us to a standard far above the one we find in the imprecatory psalms. Although God's holy standard of grace and forgiveness is difficult, shouldn't we make the attempt? Over and over, he reminds us:

"It is mine to avenge; I will repay" (Romans 12:19). There will come a day when the wrongs of this world will be righted by the Righteous One who sees all. Until that day, we are called to pour out our hurts and fears and heartbreaks to God, letting him discipline our attitudes along the way.

Until that day, perhaps we can take comfort in God's decision to include the imprecatory psalms in his word. Imperfect prayers though they were, God did not erase them from history—he still heard them. Perhaps one encouraging lesson is this: The God who transformed John, a Son of Thunder, into the Apostle of Love, is able to take even our fiercest emotions and corral them for his purposes, ultimately turning them into a reflection of his own goodness—if we will let him. None of us prays (or thinks or feels) perfectly all the time, but the more we talk to God, the more like him we will become.

Heart questions

- Are there any biblical passages that have troubled me, whether as problematic or even scandalous (slavery in the Bible, the treatment of women, the Canaanite genocide, hell, predestination)? Have I been honest, or have I ignored them, trying to forget these passages?

- How do I think it would affect outsiders to the faith to see insiders wrestling with problematic scriptures? Am I afraid it would give them an excuse to dismiss Christianity?

- Do I think it is ever appropriate for a Christian to use the weapons of the world (2 Corinthians 10:3–4)?

- How did Christ interact with his enemies? What was his heart?

- What have I learned from the imprecatory psalms?

- What does it reveal about God that he does not hide these violent, angry prayers from us? What kind of relationship does he invite us to have with him? Is God afraid of intensity or turned off by our honesty?

Prayer points

- Give me the strength of faith and integrity to admit it when there are troubling passages.

- Strengthen me with your grace to resist every impulse towards hatred, violence, and revenge.

- Enable me to live up to the high calling of holiness enjoined on us by the Lord Jesus.

---

[26] Then what about the Canaanite genocide? Deuteronomy 7:2 stipulates absolute destruction. Yet verse 1 assumes that the Jews will *drive out* the inhabitants of Canaan, not kill them. In fact, the imminent danger is accommodation to their culture, including intermarriage (v3)—a temptation that dogged the Old Testament people of God throughout their history. (Is it any different today—aren't believers tempted to intermarry with those who don't live by Christian conviction?)

A further indication that execution of Canaanites was uncommon is found in Ezra 9–10. The wives of those who were guilty of intermarriage were *not* executed. The solution is not violence, but separation. And even in the Battle of Jericho, the woman of faith was spared, along with her family (Joshua 6:25; also see Matthew 1:5!). It is often said that since sin is like gangrene, the Lord commanded Israel to deal with the pagans clinically, mercilessly. Yet Rahab was not only a Canaanite; she was an egregious sinner (a prostitute—Joshua 6:17). And so, despite the wording of the commands to destroy the Canaanites, the record—biblical as well as archaeological—indicates a different course, in line with the will of God.

10

CHRIST IN THE PSALMS, THE PSALMS IN CHRIST (PSALM 110)

In the last chapter we tackled the thorny issue of the imprecatory psalms, whose prayers are sometimes sub-Christian in attitude. They throw into high relief the topic of our current chapter. For if Psalm 109 is one of the most problematic (ugly?) Bible chapters for Christians, Psalm 110—including the most quoted passage in the New Testament—may be one of the most beautiful.

Psalms, like the rest of the Old Testament, points to the highest, purest, holiest, and fullest expression of God's will: Jesus Christ, the Word of God. And so we now turn to find Christ in the psalms.

A large number of OT passages show us Christ (like Deuteronomy 18, Isaiah 53, and Micah 5)—which shouldn't be surprising, since Jesus fulfills all three sections of the Jewish Bible: Law, Prophets, and Writings (Luke 24:44–47). Messianic passages are much more easily understood looking backward, from the perspective of Calvary, than looking forward (see 1 Peter 1:10–12).

Jesus applied the psalms to himself (like 22:1 and 31:5). This naturally leads us to messianic readings of the Psalter. As we will see, the Psalter shows us Christ in several ways. The imprecatory psalms direct us to Christ in that their spirit is so *unlike* that of Christ. They accentuate the loving spirit of Jesus all the more, and virtually shock us, driving us into his merciful arms. In terms of prophecy, however, many individual psalms point to Christ. We'll take a brief look here at the most prominent. Get ready for a lot of scripture listings in a short chapter!

> **Although we read the Old Testament *forward*, it is best understood when viewed *backward*— in the light of Calvary.**

Prophetic passages

Psalm 2:1–3, 7–8 (Acts 4:23–28, 13:33; Hebrews 1:5) shows us the begotten Son of God. Ancient Jews *paired* Psalm 2:7 and 2 Samuel 7:14, understanding them to refer to the Messiah (Matthew 1:1; Luke 1:32–33; Acts 2:29–30), the universal ruler to whom the entire world would be subject. Similar thoughts are found in 89:3, 35–36 and 132:1, all building on God's promise to David in 2 Samuel 7:11–16. Psalm 40:6–8 (Hebrews 10:5–7, quoting the Greek Old Testament[27]) gives us the incarnation. Psalm 45:6 and also 93:2 (Hebrews 1:8) show us that the Messiah is God. Psalm 102:25–27 (Hebrews 1:10–12) reveals that Christ is the eternal creator, a fact picked up on in Colossians 1:16 and other New

Testament verses. Then there's the well-known Psalm 8:3–6, a text on the sovereignty of the Messiah (echoed in Hebrews 2:8 and 1 Corinthians 15:27).

Psalm 22 contains multiple points of contact with the crucifixion of Christ, in vv1, 7–8, 16, and 18. Further, v22 indicates confidence in divine deliverance—resurrection (Hebrews 2:22). Other Psalms passages touching on Christ's passion are 31:5—committing spirit into God's hands (Luke 23:46; 1 Peter 2:23); 34:20—not a bone to be broken (John 19:32–33, 36; Exodus 12:46; Number 9:12); 35:11, 19; 69:4—malicious persons hating him without cause (John 15:24–25); 41:9 (55:12–13)—his betrayal (John 13:18); 118:22 (Isaiah 28:16; Zechariah 10:4; Matthew 21:42; Acts 4:11; 1 Peter 2:7) refers to the Messiah's rejection ("the stone the builders rejected"), while 69:8–9, 21 highlights rejection by his own family (Mark 3:21; John 7:5), consumption by zeal for God's house (John 2:17; Luke 19:45–46), and being given vinegar at the time of his crucifixion (John 19:29). Moreover, 16:8–10 is the resurrection passage Peter cites at Pentecost (Acts 2:25–28), while 68:18 is about Christ's ascension (Ephesians 4:8).

There are so many prophecies of the Messiah in Psalms, it's no wonder Jesus was able to explain his identity to the disciples on the Emmaus road by opening to them the book of Psalms, along with other parts of Scripture (Luke 24:13–35). For now, I'd like us to focus on just one psalm. (For more, I invite you to listen to two podcasts on the subject at my website.[28])

Psalm 110

¹ The LORD says to my lord:
"Sit at my right hand
   until I make your enemies
   a footstool for your feet."
² The LORD will extend your mighty scepter from Zion,
saying,
   "Rule in the midst of your enemies!". . .

⁴ The LORD has sworn
   and will not change his mind:
"You are a priest forever,
   in the order of Melchizedek."
⁵ The LORD is at your right hand:
   he will crush kings on the day of his wrath.
⁶ He will judge the nations.

Here we learn so many tremendous things about the Messiah! David refers to his descendant as his Lord. The Messiah is divine. He is to share God's throne, reigning *and* serving as priest in the order of Melchizedek. This was unheard of in Judaism: a king (who would be from the tribe of Judah) officiating as priest (from the tribe of Levi). Well, maybe not unheard of: when King Saul attempted to officiate as priest, the kingdom was taken away from him (1 Samuel 13:8–14).[29] But Jesus' priesthood is like that of Melchizedek, the priest-king of old Jerusalem (Genesis 14). Furthermore, the Messiah is Judge.

Psalm 110 is the most quoted psalm (or OT passage of any kind) in the New Testament—cited some 20 times. No wonder this is the passage Jesus—and early Christians—used with great effect to establish his Messiahship (see Matthew 22:44; Mark 12:36; Luke 20:42–43).

> **Psalm 110:1 is the most quoted OT passage in the NT—cited some 20 times.**

Christological aspects of the psalms

Clearly Psalms contains prophecies of the Messiah. But the Christ may be discerned in other ways, too. There are many ways to illustrate the fact that Jesus is divine, whether as the Word of God or as God in nature.

Psalm 1 urges us to walk in the way of the righteous; Jesus is the way (John 14:6; see Acts 24:14).

In Psalm 8, LORD, or Yahweh (YHWH), is rendered *kyrios* (Lord). The confession "Jesus is Lord" (Romans 10:9; 1 Corinthians 12:3) means he is in some way equivalent in nature with YHWH, the Lord God. How excellent is his name in all the earth! In Psalm 23, God is our shepherd; yet Jesus is the good shepherd (Ezekiel 34:10–16, 23–24, 31; Zechariah 13:7; John 10:11, 14; Hebrews 13:20; 1 Peter 5:4; Revelation 7:17)—thus the Lord Jesus is God. In Psalm 27, the Lord is our light; yet Jesus is the light (John 8:12, 9:5, 1:9, 3:19; also Matthew 5:14)—again we see that Jesus is God. In Psalm 49:7–9, 15 only God can pay the ransom for sins—no human is capable. Yet Jesus is our ransom (Matthew 20:28; Mark 10:45; 1 Timothy 2:6; Hebrews 9:15; see also Hosea 13:14)—again, implying that he is God. Or god-man—100 percent God and 100 percent man. In Psalm 55:22 and 4:8, God bears our burdens. Once again, since Jesus is our burden-bearer (Matthew 11:28–30; 1 Peter 5:7), he is God.

Jesus is God's Word, the Word become flesh (John 1:1, 14; Revelation 19:13). For dozens of related passages, see Psalm 119. And so on...again and again, the Psalter compellingly points to Jesus. In a way, Psalms serves as a bridge between the Testaments, connecting the God of the Old Testament with God in the flesh in the New Testament. Studying the messianic passages will not only strengthen your faith; it will also expand your perspective on who Jesus is—his nature, his purpose, and his glory.

Heart questions

- How familiar am I with the messianic passages in the Prophets? In the Law? If a Jewish seeker asked me to jot down a list of messianic prophecies, how many would I know off the top of my head?

- If I were a first-century Jew who knew the Scriptures (like Nicodemus), how obvious would it have been to me that Jesus was the Messiah?

- What is it about Psalms—why do I think this was the most familiar book of the Bible to first-century believing Jews and Christians?

- Do I get inspired and excited when I see Christ in the OT scriptures? Does my heart glow, my mind race, and my pulse quicken?

Prayer points

- Open my eyes that I may see Christ in the entire Bible. Let me see him clearly, neither reading too much into the text nor missing his glory in these many passages.

- Strengthen me in my knowledge of the Messianic passages, and solidify my appreciation of Christ in the psalms.

- Give me courage to live in faith on the basis of all I am learning, that I may show Christ to others.

---

[27] The Greek version of the Old Testament, called the Septuagint or LXX (because of the legend that it was translated independently and identically by 70 [LXX in Roman numerals] translators), appeared two centuries before Christ. Nearly all OT citations in the New Testament are from the LXX—which accounts for a number of differences when you compare these quotations with your English Old Testament.

[28] Visit www.douglasjacoby.com > podcasts > psalms.

[29] Another brief exception was during the intertestamental Hasmonean Dynasty, 142 BC to 55 BC.

11
SINGING IN THE SHOWER (PSALM 151)

Do you sing in the shower? Many of us do. As a new believer, I very much wanted to be able to sing like the older Christians—not tied down to a songbook. Yet I had a lot of catching up to do. So I wrote out lyrics on a piece of paper, laminated it, and hung it up in the shower. I worked on them every morning (much to the dismay of my fellow students in the dorm).

Singing is an activity natural to us all. Even my family's black border collie mix loves to sing, especially when I play the piano. (Duet for piano and canine; she's especially fond of Beethoven.) Higher mammals have deep emotions. So do many humans. (Just kidding—our dog told me to put that in.)

The Lord expects us to sing when we're happy (James 5:13), and it comes naturally to most of us. ("It" doesn't necessarily mean harmonious singing; I refer only to the act of singing—the joyful noise itself.)

My heart, O God, is steadfast;
I will sing and make music with all my soul. (Psalm 108:1)

Sometimes the singing generates the consolation; other times we sing out of our consolation. It's especially normal to sing when we appreciate our salvation. It's a kind of overflow of a relieved and grateful heart (40:1–3).

Beyond all doubt, the ancient Jews were a singing people. They sang praises to Yahweh. They sang about their hardships and dilemmas. They recounted their national history in song. Their worship was often noisy (Psalm 98:4–6, 100:1–2; 2 Samuel 6:5; 2 Chronicles 29:25–30; Ezra 3:10–13).

The Psalter spills over with singing (not counting personification, as when mountains and rivers rejoice), in Psalms 5:11; 7:17; 9:2, 11; 13:6; 18:49; 21:13; 27:6; 28:7; 30:4, 12; 32:11; 33:1, 3; 40:3; 42:8; 47:6–7; 51:14; 57:7, 9; 59:16–17; 61:8; 63:5; 65:13; 66:2, 4; 67:4; 68:4, 6, 25, 32; 69:30; 71:22–23; 75:9; 81:1; 87:7; 89:1; 90:14; 92:4; 95:1–2; 96:1–2; 98:1, 5; 100:2; 101:1; 104:33; 105:2; 106:12; 107:22; 108:1, 3; 119:54, 172; 126:2, 5–6; 132:9, 16; 135:3; 138:1, 5; 144:9; 145:7; 146:2; 147:1, 7; and 149:1, 5. Music is meant to be a thread that runs through our everyday lives.

Now did the ancient Jews really *hum* the psalms (as I claimed in chapter 2)? I was just speculating there (sorry, belated confession)—but they *could* have. Yet seriously, God's people were probably far more musical, and sang far more songs, than we imagine. Consider Solomon, that prodigy who—as long as he was doing well spiritually—made full use of both sides of his brain. He was engineer and artist, naturalist and sage. With God-given "wisdom and understanding beyond measure, and breadth of mind like the sand on the seashore," Solomon created 3000 proverbs (only a few hundred of which ended up in the book of Proverbs) and 1005 songs (1 Kings 4:29–32). One thousand and five! Undoubtedly David passed down his gift and passion for music to Solomon (1 Chronicles 23:5, 25:1; compare to 1 Kings 10:11–12 and 2 Chronicles 5:12–13). You'd think many of Solomon's songs must have ended up in the Psalter, but you'd be wrong. *Only two* (Psalms 72 and 127—less than one-fifth of one percent of his total musical output) were included. The point: We're more likely to underestimate the value of music than to overestimate it.

Since writing songs is a way to express our deepest thoughts, process our emotions, and reflect on our faith, why don't we do it more today? Of course, some people *do* write hymns, but most of us have never been brave enough to try. But why not? Give it a try! There's no pressure here, no "right way" to write a psalm—it wouldn't become Psalm 151, or be inspired—but it would be *your* psalm to God, born of the song in your heart.

And besides, there already is a 151st psalm, written long before the time of Christ, which was found among the Dead Sea Scrolls and is even included in some Orthodox Bibles.

My hands made a harp, my fingers fashioned a lyre.
And who will declare it to my Lord? The Lord himself; it is he who hears.
It was he who sent his messenger and took me from my

father's sheep,
  and anointed me with his anointing oil.
My brothers were handsome and tall,
  but the Lord was not pleased with them.
I went out to meet the Philistine, and he cursed me by his idols.
  But I drew his own sword; I beheaded him, and removed reproach from the people of Israel.[30]

This psalm isn't Scripture, but it's useful all the same, demonstrating the vigor of the Jewish musical impulse, and reminding us that creativity need not be confined to the "age of inspiration." Give psalm-writing a try as a way of opening new dimensions of your prayer life. Who knows? You may well be a budding David or Asaph!

Another way to deepen our faith musically is to memorize psalms. Choose a version that is faithful to the original, yet also "breathes." Then write it on the tablet of your heart and have it ready on your lips. Perhaps you will want to commit it to memory in another language, if you have a second tongue.[31] Discover what moves you. Let your ears take delight in the words and the rhythm. Whatever it takes—let's get into Psalms and get Psalms into us.

"It has been said that singing is the highest expression of music, perceived as the most direct expression of the emotions of the soul. If this is true, then Psalms is the most personal of all the books of the Bible. In composing the psalms, the psalmists bared their deepest sentiments and their most profound convictions. In reading the psalms, we recognize things deep within ourselves... May these ancient songs, just as they have done for ages, resonate in us—verses for the heart, music for the soul."[32]

Music has the power to transport us. It frees us from our burdens and even lifts us out of our darkness. It transfers us to the heavenly places—or more accurately, it reminds us that in some sense we are already there (Ephesians 1:3, 20; 2:6). We can even journey to Jerusalem, symbolically, as we sing the Psalms of Ascent (120–134): "For many there could be no physical journey to Zion, but the psalms allowed them to be pilgrims and festival celebrants in memory and imagination."[33]

Sing. Compose. Let your mind be full of wholesome music. Use the psalms as a model of genuine prayer. Borrow the words of the Psalter; why completely reinvent the wheel? Maybe even write your own hymn. As for me, I still sing in the shower, though not as often as I did forty years ago. The psalms remind me how much I need to get back to that. I don't know about you, but I feel a song coming on...

Heart questions

- How often do I find myself singing, lighthearted and grateful for what the Lord has done for me?

- Might it be good for me to write a psalm?

- Am I ever embarrassed to sing loud? Do I think about the words I'm singing? Do I enjoy the theology of psalms, hymns, and spiritual songs?

- Would I be willing to share a biblical psalm, or one of my own, in order to edify my brothers and sisters (1 Corinthians 14:26)?

Prayer points (adapted from Psalms)

- May I always give thanks to you for supporting me with your loving hand. When anxiety is great within me, your consolation brings me joy (94:19).

- May I remain righteous, trusting in you, O Lord, for then I know I'll have no fear of bad news (112:7).

- May my heart be not proud, Lord, nor my eyes conceited. May I not get hung up on things I don't need to concern myself with. Calm and quiet my soul, like a weaned child with its mother. May I put my hope in you, Lord, both now and forevermore (131:1–3).

---

[30] There's a longer version in the Hebrew original(s). In the LXX and in Orthodox Bibles it is Psalm 151; in the Dead Sea Scrolls, 11Q5.

[31] Psalm 1 is also the only Psalm I've ever memorized—in Hebrew. I'm mesmerized by the sound of it: *'ashrei-ha'ish asher lo' halakh ba'atsat resha'im, uvderekh chatta'im lo' 'amad, uvmoshav leitsim lo' yashav…*

[32] Rolan Monje, *Into the Psalms: Verses for the Heart, Music for the Soul* (Spring Hill, TN: DPI, 2012).

[33] Marvin E. Tate, *Word Biblical Commentary Vol. 20, Psalms 51–100*, 363.

12
OPEN MY MOUTH (PSALM 81)

In this slim volume far more psalms have been omitted than selected. Maybe that was inevitable. You may be disappointed that we didn't do justice to Psalms 8, 90, 100, 127, or your other favorites. I hope you won't hold that against me.

My hope is that this book has reignited your passion for this passionate book of the Bible, reminding you of its unique gems and inspiring you to seek more. Many capable authors have penned edifying and fruitful thoughts in a mountain of books on Psalms. At the end of this book you'll find ideas for further study. My encouragement is for us to *continue* to study Psalms, and to seek the Lord's presence. This requires interest, appetite, and character.

> *I am the LORD your God,*
> *who brought you up out of the land of Egypt.*
> *Open your mouth wide, and I will fill it.* (Psalm 81:10 ESV)

Yet sadly—as this psalm continues—Israel refused to open herself to Yahweh. If there ever comes a time when we find ourselves in such a stubborn posture, we ought to know that the Lord is there. He is always ready to fill us, but are we ready to open wide?

> *Open my eyes, that I may behold*
> *wondrous things out of your law.*
>
> (Psalm 119:18 ESV)

We must open our eyes in order to see. Yet sight and insight are not enough. Biblically speaking, having an open mouth means readiness to obey God's nourishing word (Psalm 119:11; Deuteronomy 30:14; Jeremiah 15:16).

> *I open my mouth and pant,*
> *because I long for your commandments.*
>
> (Psalm 119:131 ESV)

The psalms, like all of God's written word, invite us to "taste and see that the Lord is good" (34:8). Not only do they point us to the central figure of all history, the Lord Jesus Christ, but they are a practical resource for thriving—a vital and always-available source of spiritual refreshment and restoration.

If you chose to read this book because you found yourself spiritually adrift and needing inspiration and rejuvenation in your walk with God—wanting to thrive yet again—I pray that you have found what you sought, not in the pages of this book, but in the psalms of The Book. We all go through dry periods in our walk with God—perhaps because life has grown hard, or our hearts have grown dull, or the years have stretched long—but in those times, the Psalms can play a unique role in reawakening the very heart of our relationship with God: the passion, the prayer, the song. From that heart— that relationship—springs the will to follow, to obey, and to glorify our Father from a place of gratitude and joy. My prayer for you as you continue your study of Psalms and your lifelong journey with God is this:

May the LORD cause you to flourish,
  both you and your children.
May you be blessed by the LORD,
  the Maker of heaven and earth.

The highest heavens belong to the LORD,
  but the earth he has given to mankind.

…it is we who extol the Lord,
  both now and forevermore.

Praise the LORD. (Psalm 115:14–16, 18)

Heart questions

- Why do I read Christian books? Am I willing to seek an obedient lifestyle, rather than mere insight?

- Did I view this chapter as the *end* of my study of Psalms, or the beginning?

- Am I habitually stuck on the road to Emmaus, standing still with face downcast, and slow of heart to believe? (Luke 24:17, 25). Or am I willing to open my heart to God and "soar on wings like eagles…run and not grow weary… walk and not be faint"? (Isaiah 40:31).

Prayer points

- I am empty; fill me.

- Fill me with your spirit and with your holy word—for you have exalted above all things your name and your word.

- Thank you for putting Psalms in the Bible. You have given us permission to be real and to express ourselves with authenticity. Set my spirit free; let it soar!

Resources for Further Study of Psalms

- The Psalms podcast series, each with notes, by Douglas Jacoby (10 lessons) and Rolan Monje (8 lessons). Each lesson is suitable for a daily devotion. Visit www.douglasjacoby.com.

- *Reading, Praying & Living the Psalms* (Spring, Texas: IPI, 2005). 5 hours of audio, with 32 pages of notes.

- Rolan Monje, *Into the Psalms: Verses for the Heart, Music for the Soul* (Spring Hill, TN: DPI, 2012). A great introduction to psalms.

- Walter Brueggemann, *Praying the Psalms: Engaging Scripture and the Life of the Spirit* (Eugene, OR: Cascade, 2007). A modern classic.

- George A. F. Knight, *Psalms Volume I & II*, in The Daily Study Bible Series (Louisville: Westminster John Knox Press, 1982 and 1983). This is a practical commentary series at the basic level, similar to William Barclay's New Testament series.

- Derek Kidner, *Psalms 1–72: An Introduction & Commentary* and *Psalms 73–150: An Introduction & Commentary,* in the Tyndale Old Testament Commentaries (Downers Grove: Intervarsity Press, 1973). Intermediate level commentary series.

- C. S. Lewis, *Reflections on the Psalms* (online pdf, www.scribd .com/doc/27582307/C-S-Lewis-Reflections-on-the-Psalms). Millions have found Lewis thought-provoking.

- Peter C. Craigie, *Word Biblical Commentary Vol. 19, Psalms 1–50* (Nashville: Thomas Nelson), 1983; Marvin E. Tate, *Word Biblical Commentary Vol. 20, Psalms 51–100* (Nashville: Thomas Nelson), 1990; Leslie C. Allen, *Word Biblical Commentary Vol. 21, Psalms 101–150* (Nashville: Thomas Nelson), 2002. Advanced commentary series.

PSALMS FOR EVERY OCCASION

The following categories are not comprehensive, nor are the examples.
Rather, this table is a tool to help us realize the resources we have in the
Psalter.

All nations	67, 100, 117	Judgment	21, 62, 94
Anger	4, 10, 37	Loneliness	25, 68, 88
Anxiety	6, 13, 37	Nature	8, 19, 148
Betrayal	41, 55, 109	The needy	41, 72, 113
Christ	2, 22, 110	Old age	37, 71, 90
Close to God	62, 63, 84	Opposition	3, 54, 56
Confession	32, 38, 51	Orphans	10, 82, 146
Confidence	18, 27, 34	Overwhelmed	61, 69, 142
Creation	19, 104, 148	Politics	20, 82, 146
Decisions	1, 25, 27	Praise	145, 148, 150
Depression	13, 42, 43	Prayer	4, 5, 55
Disaster	46, 74, 91	Protection	20, 91, 121
Distress	3, 39, 54	Providence	90, 104, 139
Eternity	17, 73, 90	Purity of heart	19, 139, 141
Family	127, 128, 144	Repentance	32, 51, 90
Fear	3, 27, 46	Rescue	40, 107, 116
Feeling faint	61, 142, 143	Sickness	6, 38, 41
Forgiveness	32, 103, 130	Sin	32, 36, 38
Fresh start	30, 40, 51	Singing	96, 98, 108
God (attributes)	8, 100, 103	Sovereignty	33, 47, 115
Guidance	23, 25, 140	Thanksgiving	100, 107, 118
Heaven	16, 17, 49	Time with God	42, 84, 63
Holiness	15, 24, 99	Unity	33, 122, 133
Hope	25, 123, 131	Wavering	37, 73, 78
Humility	25, 95, 131	Wisdom	1, 90, 111
Integrity	26, 101, 141	The world	12, 14, 120
Israel's history	78, 106, 136	Victory	18, 34, 144
Jerusalem	48, 87, 122	Worship	99, 138, 147
Joy	30, 33, 95	Zeal	18, 69, 119

Here are my favorite Psalms (suggested for memorization):

1:1-6	**40**:2-3	**86**:4-6, 10-12	**119**:4-6, 9-12, 16, 18,
5:3	**42**:2	**90**:8, 10, 12	29, 32, 34-37, 60, 64,
6:3	**46**:10	**92**:14	66-68, 71-72, 79-80,
7:11	**48**:12-14	**93**:5	93, 97, 105, 111-112,
12:6-8	**49**:16-20	**94**:12, 19	120, 131, 133, 162,
17:15	**51**:1-19	**100**:1-5	175-176
18:2, 28	**55**:22	**101**:2-4	**120**:7
19:7-14	**56**:11	**103**:2, 8-13, 19	**127**:1-5
20:7	**57**:5, 11	**105**:4	**130**:3-4
23:1-6	**61**:2	**107**:9	**131**:1-3
25:21	**62**:5, 8, 10	**109**:4	**133**:1-3
26:11-12	**63**:2-3, 8	**111**:2-3, 9-10	**138**:2
27:14	**65**:2	**112**:7	**139**:17, 23-24
28:7	**68**:6, 19	**113**:7	**141**:3-5
31:5, 24	**69**:6, 9	**115**:1, 3	**143**:2, 6, 10
32:2-3	**71**:3, 17-18, 20	**116**:15	**145**:3-5, 8-9, 18
34:5, 8, 18-19	**72**:18-19	**117**:1-2	**147**:3, 5-6, 10-11
36:2	**73**:24-28	**118**:22-24	**149**:4
37:4-5, 31	**84**:1-12		

THANKS

Thanks are due to a number of friends who have kindly looked over the manuscript. Some found blatant errors. Others made suggestions for rephrasing, where my expression was awkward or unclear. Still others kept me motivated by encouraging me to "keep it real." Those who deserve credit include:

David Anderson, Sandy Anjilivelil, Daniel Braucher, Nick and Laura Cotton, Mike DeSouza, Michelle Diekmeyer, Geoff Fawcett, Greg Fender, Matt FitzGibbon, Bill Goshorn, Fred Haight, John Hanes, Joey Harris, Randy Harris, John Hoyt, Ben Hutchings, Tom Jones, Don Lee, Sherwin Mackintosh, Rolan Monje, Kelli Reinhardt, Wouter and Sara Roux, Lisa Sawhill, Ana Maria Schirmer, Lois Schmitt, Joe Sciortino, Eric and Paulette Sifford, and Bobbye Trotter.

Those who labored especially hard on the book are my editors Elizabeth Thompson and Amy Morgan.

If I left anyone out—which I fear I may have—please shoot me an email and this will be corrected in the second printing. Even if modesty would prevent you from jogging my memory, I'd be saddened for the oversight, given my debt to you.

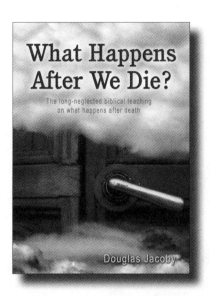

What happens after we die? There are few questions more universal than this. We all want to know what happens when we die. No matter our religion, culture, or social status, no one is indifferent about death.

But exactly what happens the instant we die? Is there a second chance for those who did not turn to the Lord during their earthly lives? Do we become angels, floating up in the clouds, or ghosts, restlessly roaming the earth? Do we go down a tunnel of light? Are people even conscious of what happens between death and Judgment Day, or does our soul simply go to sleep? Do we go straight to heaven, and keep an eye on our friends and family still on earth?

In this book you'll find surprising insights into what the Bible teaches about the afterlife.

What Happens After We Die?
Douglas Jacoby
Available at www.ipibooks.com

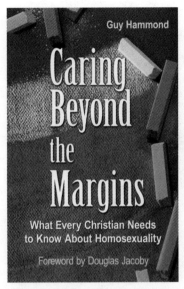

Guy Hammond

Caring Beyond the Margins

What Every Christian Needs to Know About Homosexuality

Foreword by Douglas Jacoby

Guy Hammond is the founder and executive director of **Strength in Weakness Ministries**, whose aim is to train Christian leaders and members alike to work compassionately with those who are same-gender attracted. In *Caring Beyond the Margins: What Every Christian Needs to Know About Homosexuality*, you will benefit from the wisdom and life experiences of one who personally shares in the journey of those who truly do strive for "strength in weakness" (see 2 Corinthians 12:9).

In a nutshell there are four transformational truths you will learn in this book: First, while living a life of active homosexuality is sinful, simply being attracted to the same gender is not. Second, the primary goal of the same-sex-attracted disciple is not to become heterosexually attracted, but to live a life of holiness. Third, God is not ashamed or embarrassed of same-sex-attracted Christians. Their value and worth to him and his church are not based on that criterion. Last, every same-sex-attracted follower of Jesus can absolutely live a successful Christian life that God would be incredibly proud of, whether or not their homoerotic appealings ever disappear.

Caring Beyond the Margins
Guy Hammond
Available at www.ipibooks.com

The mission of the International Bible Teaching Ministry is to make us think about faith. At www.douglasjacoby.com you will find articles, weekly podcasts, Q&As and much more—nearly 10,000 pages of Christian resources for you and your friends. Trekking through the exciting terrain of God's word is deeply fulfilling. Enjoy the adventure.

Illumination Publishers

For the best in Christian writing and audio instruction, go to www.
ipibooks.com. We're dedicated to producing in-depth teaching
that will inform, inspire and encourage Christians to a deeper
and more committed walk with God. You can email us from the
website or reach us at (832)-559-3658.

www.ipibooks.com